The Marquise de Brinvilliers

Alexandre Dumas

The Marquise De Brinvilliers

Towards the end of the year 1665, on a fine autumn evening, there was a considerable crowd assembled on the Pont-Neuf where it makes a turn down to the rue Dauphine. The object of this crowd and the centre of attraction was a closely shut, carriage. A police official was trying to force open the door, and two out of the four sergeants who were with him were holding the horses back and the other two stopping the driver, who paid no attention to their commands, but only endeavoured to urge his horses to a gallop. The struggle had been going on same time, when suddenly one of the doors violentiy pushed open, and a young officer in the uniform of a cavalry captain jumped down, shutting the door as he did so though not too quickly for the nearest spectators to perceive a woman sitting at the back of the carriage. She was wrapped in cloak and veil, and judging by the precautions she, had taken to hide her face from every eye, she must have had her reasons for avoiding recognition.

"Sir," said the young man, addressing the officer with a haughty air, "I presume, till I find myself mistaken, that your business is with me alone; so I will ask you to inform me what powers you may have for thus stopping my coach; also, since I have alighted, I desire you to give your men orders to let the vehicle go on."

"First of all," replied the man, by no means intimidated by these lordly airs, but signing to his men that they must not release the coach or the horses, "be so good as to answer my questions."

"I am attending," said the young man, controlling his agitation by a visible effort.

"Are you the Chevalier Gaudin de Sainte-Croix?"

"I am he."

"Captain of the Tracy, regiment?"

1

"Yes, sir."

"Then I arrest you in the king's name."

"What powers have you?" This warrant."

Sainte-Croix cast a rapid glance at the paper, and instantly recognised the signature of the minister of police: he then apparently confined his attention to the woman who was still in the carriage; then he returned to his first question.

"This is all very well, sir," he said to the officer, "but this warrant contains no other name than mine, and so you have no right to expose thus to the public gaze the lady with whom I was travelling when you arrested me. I must beg of you to order your assistants to allow this carriage to drive on; then take me where you please, for I am ready to go with you."

To the officer this request seemed a just one: he signed to his men to let the driver and the horses go on; and, they, who had waited only for this, lost no time in breaking through the crowd, which melted away before them; thus the woman escaped for whose safety the prisoner seemed so much concerned.

Sainte-Croix kept his promise and offered no resistance; for some moments he followed the officer, surrounded by a crowd which seemed to have transferred all its curiosity to his account; then, at the corner of the Quai de d'Horloge, a man called up a carriage that had not been observed before, and Sainte-Croix took his place with the same haughty and disdainful air that he had shown throughout the scene we have just described. The officer sat beside him, two of his men got up behind, and the other two, obeying no doubt their master's orders, retired with a parting direction to the driver,

"The Bastille!"

Our readers will now permit us to make them more fully acquainted with the man who is to take the first place in the story. The origin of

Gaudin de Sainte-Croix was not known: according to one tale, he was the natural son of a great lord; another account declared that he was the offspring of poor people, but that, disgusted with his obscure birth, he preferred a splendid disgrace, and therefore chose to pass for what he was not. The only certainty is that he was born at Montauban, and in actual rank and position he was captain of the Tracy regiment. At the time when this narrative opens, towards the end of 1665, Sainte-Croix was about twenty-eight or thirty, a fine young man of cheerful and lively appearance, a merry comrade at a banquet, and an excellent captain: he took his pleasure with other men, and was so impressionable a character that he enjoyed a virtuous project as well as any plan for a debauch; in love he was most susceptible, and jealous to the point of madness even about a courtesan, had she once taken his fancy; his prodigality was princely, although he had no income; further, he was most sensitive to slights, as all men are who, because they are placed in an equivocal position, fancy that everyone who makes any reference to their origin is offering an intentional insult.

We must now see by what a chain of circumstances he had arrived at his present position. About the year 1660, Sainte-Croix, while in the army, had made the acquaintance of the Marquis de Brinvilliers, maitre-de-camp of the Normandy regiment.

Their age was much the same, and so was their manner of life: their virtues and their vices were similar, and thus it happened that a mere acquaintance grew into a friendship, and on his return from the field the marquis introduced Sainte-Croix to his wife, and he became an intimate of the house. The usual results followed. Madame de Brinvilliers was then scarcely eight-and-twenty: she had married the marquis in 1651-that is, nine years before. He enjoyed an income of 30,000 livres, to which she added her dowry of 200,000 livres, exclusive of her expectations in the future. Her name was Marie-Madeleine; she had a sister and two brothers: her father, M. de Dreux d'Aubray; was civil lieutenant at the Chatelet de Paris. At the age of twenty-eight the marquise was at the height of her beauty: her figure was small but perfectly proportioned; her rounded face was charmingly pretty; her features, so regular that no emotion seemed to alter their beauty, suggested the lines of a statue miraculously endowed with life: it was easy enough to mistake for the repose of a happy conscience the cold, cruel calm which served as a mask to cover remorse.

Sainte-Croix and the marquise loved at first sight, and she was soon his mistress. The marquis, perhaps endowed with the conjugal philosophy which alone pleased the taste of the period, perhaps too much occupied with his own pleasure to see what was going on before his eyes, offered no jealous obstacle to the intimacy, and continued his foolish extravagances long after they had impaired his fortunes: his affairs became so entangled that the marquise, who cared for him no longer, and desired a fuller liberty for the indulgence of her new passion, demanded and obtained a separation. She then left her husband's house, and henceforth abandoning all discretion, appeared everywhere in public with Sainte-Croix. This behaviour, authorised as it was by the example of the highest nobility, made no impression upon the. Marquis of Brinvilliers,who merrily pursued the road to ruin, without worrying about his wife's behaviour. Not so M. de Dreux d'Aubray: he had the scrupulosity of a legal dignitary. He was scandalised at his daughter's conduct, and feared a stain upon his own fair name: he procured a warrant for the arrest of Sainte-Croix wheresoever the bearer might chance to encounter him. We have seen how it was put in execution when Sainte-Croix was driving in the carriage of the marquise, whom our readers will doubtless have recognised as the woman who concealed herself so carefully.

>From one's knowledge of the character of Sainte-Croix, it is easy to imagine that he had to use great self-control to govern the anger he felt at being arrested in the middle of the street; thus, although during the whole drive he uttered not a single word, it was plain to see that a terrible storm was gathering, soon to break. But he preserved the same impossibility both at the opening and shutting of the fatal gates, which, like the gates of hell, had so often bidden those who entered abandon all hope on their threshold, and again when he replied to the formal questions put to him by the governor. His voice was calm, and when they gave him they prison register he signed it

with a steady hand. At once a gaoler, taking his orders from the governor, bade him follow: after traversing various corridors, cold and damp, where the daylight might sometimes enter but fresh air never, he opened a door, and Sainte-Croix had no sooner entered than he heard it locked behind him.

At the grating of the lock he turned. The gaoler had left him with no light but the rays of the moon, which, shining through a barred window some eight or ten feet from the ground, shed a gleam upon a miserable truckle-bed and left the rest of the room in deep obscurity. The prisoner stood still for a moment and listened; then, when he had heard the steps die away in the distance and knew himself to be alone at last, he fell upon the bed with a cry more like the roaring of a wild beast than any human sound: he cursed his fellow- man who had snatched him from his joyous life to plunge him into a dungeon; he cursed his God who had let this happen; he cried aloud to whatever powers might be that could grant him revenge and liberty.

Just at that moment, as though summoned by these words from the bowels of the earth, a man slowly stepped into the circle of blue light that fell from the window-a man thin and pale, a man with long hair, in a black doublet, who approached the foot of the bed where Sainte-Croix lay. Brave as he was, this apparition so fully answered to his prayers (and at the period the power of incantation and magic was still believed in) that he felt no doubt that the arch-enemy of the human race, who is continually at hand, had heard him and had now come in answer to his prayers. He sat up on the bed, feeling mechanically at the place where the handle of his sword would have been but two hours since, feeling his hair stand on end, and a cold sweat began to stream down his face as the strange fantastic being step by step approached him. At length the apparition paused, the prisoner and he stood face to face for a moment, their eyes riveted; then the mysterious stranger spoke in gloomy tones.

"Young man," said he, "you have prayed to the devil for vengeance on the men who have taken you, for help against the God who has abandoned you. I have the means, and I am here to proffer it. Have you the courage to accept?"

"First of all," asked Sainte-Croix; "who are you?"

"Why seek you to know who I am," replied the unknown, "at the very moment when I come at your call, and bring what you desire?"

"All the same," said Sainte-Croix, still attributing what he heard to a supernatural being, "when one makes a compact of this kind, one prefers to know with whom one is treating."

"Well, since you must know," said the stranger, "I am the Italian Exili."

Sainte-Croix shuddered anew, passing from a supernatural vision to a horrible reality. The name he had just heard had a terrible notoriety at the time, not only in France but in Italy as well. Exili had been driven out of Rome, charged with many poisonings, which, however, could not be satisfactorily brought home to him. He had gone to Paris, and there, as in his native country, he had drawn the eyes of the authorities upon himself; but neither in Paris nor in Rome was he, the pupil of Rene and of Trophana, convicted of guilt. All the same, though proof was wanting, his enormities were so well accredited that there was no scruple as to having him arrested. A warrant was out against him: Exili was taken up, and was lodged in the Bastille. He had been there about six months when Sainte-Croix was brought to the same place. The prisoners were numerous just then, so the governor had his new guest put up in the same room as the old one, mating Exili and Sainte-Croix, not knowing that they were a pair of demons. Our readers now understand the rest. Sainte-Croix was put into an unlighted room by the gaoler, and in the dark had failed to see his companion: he had abandoned himself to his rage, his imprecations had revealed his state of mind to Exili, who at once seized the occasion for gaining a devoted and powerful disciple, who once out of prison might open the doors for him, perhaps, or at least avenge his fate should he be incarcerated for life.

The repugnance felt by Sainte-Croix for his fellow-prisoner did ,not last long, and the clever master found his pupil apt. Sainte-Croix, a strange mixture of qualities good and evil, had reached the supreme crisis of his life, when the powers of darkness or of light were to prevail. Maybe, if he had met some angelic soul at this point, he would have been led to God; he encountered a demon, who conducted him to Satan.

Exili was no vulgar poisoner: he was a great artist in poisons, comparable with the Medici or the Borgias. For him murder was a fine art, and he had reduced it to fixed and rigid rules: he had arrived at a point when he was guided not by his personal interest but by a taste for experiment. God has reserved the act of creation for Himself, but has suffered destruction to be within the scope of man: man therefore supposes that in destroying life he is God's equal. Such was the nature of Exili's pride: he was the dark, pale alchemist of death: others might seek the mighty secret of life, but he had found the secret of destruction.

For a time Sainte-Croix hesitated: at last he yielded to the taunts of his companion, who accused Frenchmen of showing too much honour in their crimes, of allowing themselves to be involved in the ruin of their enemies, whereas they might easily survive them and triumph over their destruction. In opposition to this French gallantry, which often involves the murderer in a death more cruel than that he has given, he pointed to the Florentine traitor with his amiable smile and his deadly poison. He indicated certain powders and potions, some of them of dull action, wearing out the victim so slowly that he dies after long suffering; others violent and so quick, that they kill like a flash of lightning, leaving not even time for a single cry. Little by little Sainte-Croix became interested in the ghastly science that puts the lives of all men in the hand of one. He joined in Exili's experiments; then he grew clever enough to make them for himself; and when, at the year's end, he left the Bastille, the pupil was almost as accomplished as his master.

Sainte-Croix returned into that society which had banished him, fortified by a fatal secret by whose aid he could repay all the evil he had received. Soon afterwards Exili was set free—how it happened is not known—and sought out Sainte-Croix, who let him a room in the name of his steward, Martin de Breuille, a room situated in the blind, alley off the Place Maubert, owned by a woman called Brunet.

It is not known whether Sainte-Croix had an opportunity of seeing the Marquise de Brinvilliers during his sojourn in the Bastille, but it is certain that as soon as he was a free man the lovers were more attached than ever. They had learned by experience, however, of what they had to fear; so they resolved that they would at once make trial of Sainte-Croix's newly acquired knowledge, and M. d'Aubray was selected by his daughter for the first victim. At one blow she would free herself from the inconvenience of his rigid censorship, and by inheriting his goods would repair her own fortune, which had been almost dissipated by her husband. But in trying such a bold stroke one must be very sure of results, so the marquise decided to experiment beforehand on another person. Accordingly, when one day after luncheon her maid, Francoise Roussel, came into her room, she gave her a slice of mutton and some preserved gooseberries for her own meal. The girl unsuspiciously ate what her mistress gave her, but almost at once felt ill, saying she had severe pain in the stomach, and a sensation as though her heart were being pricked with pins. But she did not die, and the marquise perceived that the poison needed to be made stronger, and returned it to Sainte-Croix, who brought her some more in a few days' time.

The moment had come for action. M. d'Aubray, tired with business, was to spend a holiday at his castle called Offemont. The marquise offered to go with him. M. d'Aubray, who supposed her relations with Sainte-Croix to be quite broken off, joyfully accepted. Offemont was exactly the place for a crime of this nature. In the middle of the forest of Aigue, three or four miles from Compiegne, it would be impossible to get efficient help before the rapid action of the poison had made it useless.

M. d'Aubray started with his daughter and one servant only. Never had the marquise been so devoted to her father, so especially attentive, as she was during this journey. And M. d'Aubray, like

Christ—who though He had no children had a father's heart—loved his repentant daughter more than if she had never strayed. And then the marquise profited by the terrible calm look which we have already noticed in her face: always with her father, sleeping in a room adjoining his, eating with him, caring for his comfort in every way, thoughtful and affectionate, allowing no other person to do anything for him, she had to present a smiling face, in which the most suspicious eye could detect nothing but filial tenderness, though the vilest projects were in her heart. With this mask she one evening offered him some soup that was poisoned. He took it; with her eyes she saw him put it to his lips, watched him drink it down, and with a brazen countenance she gave no outward sign of that terrible anxiety that must have been pressing on her heart. When he had drunk it all, and she had taken with steady hands the cup and its saucer, she went back to her own room, waited and listened....

The effect was rapid. The marquise heard her father moan; then she heard groans. At last, unable to endure his sufferings, he called out to his daughter. The marquise went to him. But now her face showed signs of the liveliest anxiety, and it was for M. d'Aubray to try to reassure her about himself! He thought it was only a trifling indisposition, and was not willing that a doctor should be disturbed. But then he was seized by a frightful vomiting, followed by such unendurable pain that he yielded to his daughter's entreaty that she should send for help. A doctor arrived at about eight o'clock in the morning, but by that time all that could have helped a scientific inquiry had been disposed of: the doctor saw nothing, in M.d'Aubray's story but what might be accounted for by indigestion; so he dosed him, and went back to Compiegne.

All that day the marquise never left the sick man. At night she had a bed made up in his room, declaring that no one else must sit up with him; thus she, was able to watch the progress of the malady and see with her own eyes the conflict between death and life in the body of her father. The next day the doctor came again: M. d'Aubray was worse; the nausea had ceased, but the pains in the stomach were now more acute; a strange fire seemed to burn his vitals; and a treatment was ordered which necessitated his return to Paris. He was soon so weak that he thought it might be best to go only so far as Compiegne, but the marquise was so insistent as to the necessity for further and better advice than anything he could get away from home, that M. d'Aubray decided to go. He made the journey in his own carriage, leaning upon his daughter's shoulder; the behaviour of the marquise was always the same: at last M. d'Aubray reached Paris. All had taken place as the marquise desired; for the scene was now changed: the doctor who had witnessed the symptoms would not be present at the death; no one could discover the cause by studying the progress of the disorder; the thread of investigation was snapped in two, and the two ends were now too distant to be joined again. In spite, of every possible attention, M. d'Aubray grew continually worse; the marquise was faithful to her mission, and never left him for an hour. At list, after four days of agony, he died in his daughter's arms, blessing the woman who was his murderess. Her grief then broke forth uncontrolled. Her sobs and tears were so vehement that her brothers' grief seemed cold beside hers. Nobody suspected a crime, so no autopsy was held; the tomb was closed, and not the slightest suspicion had approached her.

But the marquise had only gained half her purpose. She had now more freedom for her love affairs, but her father's dispositions were not so favourable as she expected: the greater part of his property, together with his business, passed to the elder brother and to the second brother, who was Parliamentary councillor; the position of, the marquise was very little improved in point of fortune.

Sainte-Croix was leading a fine and joyous life. Although nobody supposed him to be wealthy, he had a steward called Martin, three lackeys called George, Lapierre, and Lachaussee, and besides his coach and other carriages he kept ordinary bearers for excursions at night. As he was young and good-looking, nobody troubled about where all these luxuries came from. It was quite the custom in those days that a well-set-up young gentleman should want for nothing, and Sainte-Croix was commonly said to have found the philosopher's stone. In his life in the world he had formed friendships with various persons, some noble, some rich: among the latter was a man named Reich de Penautier, receiver-general of the clergy and treasurer of the States of Languedoc, a millionaire, and one of those men who are always successful, and who seem able by the help of their money to arrange matters that would appear to be in the province of God alone. This Penautier was connected in business with a man called d'Alibert, his first clerk, who died all of a sudden of apoplexy. The attack was known to Penautier sooner than to his own family: then the papers about the conditions of partnership disappeared, no one knew how, and d'Alibert's wife and child were ruined. D'Alibert's brother-in-law, who was Sieur de la Magdelaine, felt certain vague suspicions concerning this death, and wished to get to the bottom of it; he accordingly began investigations, which were suddenly brought to an end by his death.

In one way alone Fortune seemed to have abandoned her favourite: Maitre Penautier had a great desire to succeed the Sieur of Mennevillette, who was receiver of the clergy, and this office was worth nearly 60,000 livres. Penautier knew that Mennevillette was retiring in favour of his chief clerk, Messire Pierre Hannyvel, Sieur de Saint-Laurent, and he had taken all the necessary, steps for buying the place over his head: the Sieur de Saint-Laurent, with the full support of the clergy, obtained the reversion for nothing—a thing that never happened before. Penautier then offered him 40,000 crowns to go halves, but Saint-Laurent refused. Their relations, however, were not broken off, and they continued to meet. Penautier was considered such a lucky fellow that it was generally expected he would somehow or other get some day the post he coveted so highly. People who had no faith in the mysteries of alchemy declared that Sainte-Croix and Penautier did business together.

Now, when the period for mourning was over, the relations of the marquise and Sainte-Croix were as open and public as before: the two brothers d'Aubray expostulated with her by the medium of an older sister who was in a Carmelite nunnery, and the marquise perceived that her father had on his death bequeathed the care and supervision of her to her brothers. Thus her first crime had been all but in vain: she had wanted to get rid of her father's rebukes and to gain his fortune; as a fact the fortune was diminished by reason of her elder brothers, and she had scarcely enough to pay her debts;

while the rebukes were renewed from the mouths of her brothers, one of whom, being civil lieutenant, had the power to separate her again from her lover. This must be prevented. Lachaussee left the service of Sainte-Croix, and by a contrivance of the marquise was installed three months later as servant of the elder brother, who lived with the civil lieutenant. The poison to be used on this occasion was not so swift as the one taken by M. d'Aubray so violent a death happening so soon in the same family might arouse suspicion. Experiments were tried once more, not on animals—for their different organisation might put the poisoner's science in the wrong—but as before upon human subjects; as before, a 'corpus vili' was taken. The marquise had the reputation of a pious and charitable lady; seldom did she fail to relieve the poor who appealed: more than this, she took part in the work of those devoted women who are pledged to the service of the sick, and she walked the hospitals and presented wine and other medicaments. No one was surprised when she appeared in her ordinary way at l'Hotel-Dieu. This time she brought biscuits and cakes for the convalescent patients, her gifts being, as usual, gratefully received. A month later she paid another visit, and inquired after certain patients in whom she was particularly interested: since the last time she came they had suffered a relapse—the malady had changed in nature, and had shown graver symptoms. It was a kind of deadly fatigue, killing them by a slows strange decay. She asked questions of the doctors but could learn nothing: this malady was unknown to them, and defied all the resources of their art. A fortnight later she returned. Some of the sick people were dead, others still alive, but desperately ill; living skeletons, all that seemed left of them was sight, speech, and breath. At the end of two months they were all dead, and the physicians had been as much at a loss over the post-mortems as over the treatment of the dying.

Experiments of this kind were reassuring; so Lachaussee had orders to carry out his instructions. One day the civil lieutenant rang his bell, and Lachaussee, who served the councillor, as we said before, came up for orders. He found the lieutenant at work with his secretary, Couste what he wanted was a glass of wine and water. In a moment Lachaussee brought it in. The lieutenant put the glass to his lips, but at the first sip pushed it away, crying, "What have you brought, you wretch? I believe you want to poison me." Then handing the glass to his secretary, he added, "Look at it, Couste: what is this stuff?" The secretary put a few drops into a coffee-spoon, lifting it to his nose and then to his mouth: the drink had the smell and taste of vitriol. Meanwhile Lachaussee went up to the secretary and told him he knew what it must be: one of the councillor's valets had taken a dose of medicine that morning, and without noticing he must have brought the very glass his companion had used. Saying this, he took the glass from the secretary's hand, put it to his lips, pretending to taste it himself, and then said he had no doubt it was so, for he recognised the smell. He then threw the wine into the fireplace.

As the lieutenant had not drunk enough to be upset by it, he soon forgot this incident and the suspicions that had been aroused at the moment in his mind. Sainte-Croix and the marquise perceived that they had made a false step, and at the risk of involving several people in their plan for vengeance, they decided on the employment of other means. Three months passed without any favourable occasion presenting itself; at last, on one of the early days of April 1670, the lieutenant took his brother to his country place, Villequoy, in Beauce, to spend the Easter vacation. Lachaussee was with his master, and received his instructions at the moment of departure.

The day after they arrived in the country there was a pigeon-pie for dinner: seven persons who had eaten it felt indisposed after the meal, and the three who had not taken it were perfectly well. Those on whom the poisonous substance had chiefly acted were the lieutenant, the councillor, and the commandant of the watch. He may have eaten more, or possibly the poison he had tasted on the former occasion helped, but at any rate the lieutenant was the first to be attacked with vomiting two hours later, the councillor showed the same symptoms; the commandant and the others were a prey for several hours to frightful internal pains; but from the beginning their condition was not nearly so grave as that of the two brothers. This time again, as usual, the help of doctors was useless. On the 12th of April, five days after they had been poisoned, the lieutenant and his brother returned to Paris so changed that anyone would have thought they had both suffered a long and cruel illness. Madame de Brinvilliers was in the country at the time, and did not come back during the whole time that her brothers were ill. From the very first consultation in the lieutenant's case the doctors entertained no hope. The symptoms were the same as those to which his father had succumbed, and they supposed it was an unknown disease in the family. They gave up all hope of recovery. Indeed, his state grew worse and worse; he felt an unconquerable aversion for every kind of food, and the vomiting was incessant. The last three days of his life he complained that a fire was burning in his breast, and the flames that burned within seemed to blaze forth at his eyes, the only part of his body that appeared to live, so like a corpse was all the rest of him. On the 17th of June 1670 he died: the poison had taken seventy-two days to complete its work. Suspicion began to dawn: the lieutenant's body was opened, and a formal report was drawn up. The operation was performed in the presence of the surgeons Dupre and Durant, and Gavart, the apothecary, by M. Bachot, the brothers' private physician. They found the stomach and duodenum to be black and falling to pieces, the liver burnt and gangrened. They said that this state of things must have been produced by poison, but as the presence of certain bodily humours sometimes produces similar appearances, they durst not declare that the lieutenant's death could not have come about by natural causes, and he was buried without further inquiry.

It was as his private physician that Dr. Bachot had asked for the autopsy of his patient's brother. For the younger brother seemed to have been attacked by the same complaint, and the doctor hoped to find from the death of the one some means for preserving the life of the other. The councillor was in a violent fever, agitated unceasingly both in body and mind: he could not bear any position of any kind for more than a few minutes at a time. Bed was a place of torture; but if he got up, he cried for it again, at least for a change of suffering. At the end of three months he died. His stomach, duodenum, and liver were all in the same corrupt state as his brother's, and more than that, the surface of his body was burnt away. This, said the doctors; was no dubious sign of poisoning; although, they added, it sometimes happened that a 'cacochyme' produced the same effect. Lachaussee was so far from being suspected, that the councillor, in recognition of the care he had bestowed on him in his last illness, left him in his will a legacy of a hundred crowns; moreover, he received a thousand francs from Sainte-Croix and the marquise.

So great a disaster in one family, however, was not only sad but alarming. Death knows no hatred: death is deaf and blind, nothing more, and astonishment was felt at this ruthless destruction of all who bore one name. Still nobody suspected the true culprits, search was fruitless, inquiries led nowhere: the marquise put on mourning for her brothers, Sainte-Croix continued in his path of folly, and all things went on as before. Meanwhile Sainte-Croix had made the acquaintance of the Sieur de Saint Laurent, the same man from whom Penautier had asked for a post without success, and had made friends with him. Penautier had meanwhile become the heir of his father-in- law, the Sieur Lesecq, whose death had most unexpectedly occurred; he had thereby gained a second post in Languedoc and an immense property: still, he coveted the place of receiver of the clergy. Chance now once more helped him: a few days after taking over from Sainte-Croix a man-servant named George, M. de Saint-Laurent fell sick, and his illness showed symptoms similar to those observed in the case of the d'Aubrays, father and sons; but it was more rapid, lasting only twenty-four hours. Like them, M. de Saint-Laurent died a prey to frightful tortures. The same day an officer from the sovereign's court came to see him, heard every detail connected with his friend's death, and when told of the symptoms said before the servants to Sainfray the notary that it would be necessary to examine the body. An hour later George disappeared, saying nothing to anybody, and not even asking for his wages. Suspicions were excited; but again they remained vague. The autopsy showed a state of things not precisely to be called peculiar to poisoning cases the intestines, which the fatal poison had not had time to burn as in the case of the d'Aubrays, were marked with reddish spots like flea- bites. In June Penautier obtained the post that had been held by the Sieur de Saint-Laurent.

But the widow had certain suspicions which were changed into something like certainty by George's flight. A particular circumstance aided and almost confirmed her doubts. An abbe who was a friend of her husband, and knew all about the disappearance of George, met him some days afterwards in the rue des Masons, near the Sorbonne. They were both on the same side, and a hay-cart coming along the street was causing a block. George raised his head and saw the abbe, knew him as a friend of his late master, stooped under the cart and crawled to the other side, thus at the risk of being crushed escaping from the eyes of a man whose appearance recalled his crime and inspired him with fear of punishment. Madame de Saint-Laurent preferred a charge against George, but though he was sought for everywhere, he could never be found. Still the report of these strange deaths, so sudden and so incomprehensible, was bruited about Paris, and people began to feel frightened. Sainte-Croix, always in the gay world, encountered the talk in drawing-rooms, and began to feel a little uneasy. True, no suspicion pointed as yet in his direction; but it was as well to take precautions, and Sainte-Croix began to consider how he could be freed from anxiety. There was a post in the king's service soon to be vacant, which would cost 100,000 crowns; and although Sainte-Croix had no apparent means, it was rumoured that he was about to purchase it. He first addressed himself to Belleguise to treat about this affair with Penautier. There was some difficulty, however, to be encountered in this quarter. The sum was a large one, and Penautier no longer required help; he had already come into all the inheritance he looked for, and so he tried to throw cold water on the project.

Sainte-Croix thus wrote to Belleguise:

> "DEAR FRIEND,—Is it possible that you need any more talking to about the matter you know of, so important as it is, and, maybe, able to give us peace and quiet for the rest of our days! I really think the devil must be in it, or else you simply will not be sensible: do show your common sense, my good man, and look at it from all points of view; take it at its very worst, and you still ought to feel bound to serve me, seeing how I have made everything all right for you: all

our interests are together in this matter. Do help me, I beg of you; you may feel sure I shall be deeply grateful, and you will never before have acted so agreeably both for me and for yourself. You know quite enough about it, for I have not spoken so openly even to my own brother as I have to you. If you can come this afternoon, I shall be either at the house or quite near at hand, you know where I mean, or I will expect you tomorrow morning, or I will come and find you, according to what you reply.—Always yours with all my heart."

The house meant by Sainte-Croix was in the rue des Bernardins, and the place near at hand where he was to wait for Belleguise was the room he leased from the widow Brunet, in the blind alley out of the Place Maubert. It was in this room and at the apothecary Glazer's that Sainte-Croix made his experiments; but in accordance with poetical justice, the manipulation of the poisons proved fatal to the workers themselves. The apothecary fell ill and died; Martin was attacked by fearful sickness, which brought, him to death's door. Sainte-Croix was unwell, and could not even go out, though he did not know what was the matter. He had a furnace brought round to his house from Glazer's, and ill as he was, went on with the experiments. Sainte-Croix was then seeking to make a poison so subtle that the very effluvia might be fatal. He had heard of the poisoned napkin given to the young dauphin, elder brother of Charles VII, to wipe his hands on during a game of tennis, and knew that the contact had caused his death; and the still discussed tradition had informed him of the gloves of Jeanne d'Albret; the secret was lost, but Sainte- Croix hoped to recover it. And then there happened one of those strange accidents which seem to be not the hand of chance but a punishment from Heaven. At the very moment when Sainte-Croix was bending over his furnace, watching the fatal preparation as it became hotter and hotter, the glass mask which he wore over his face as a protection from any poisonous exhalations that might rise up from the mixture, suddenly dropped off, and Sainte-Croix dropped to the ground as though felled by a lightning stroke. At supper-time, his wife finding that he did not come out from his closet where he was shut in, knocked at the door, and received no answer; knowing that her husband was wont to busy himself with dark and mysterious matters, she feared some disaster had occurred. She called her servants, who broke in the door. Then she found Sainte-Croix stretched out beside the furnace, the broken glass lying by his side. It was impossible to deceive the public as to the circumstances of this strange and sudden death: the servants had seen the corpse, and they talked. The commissary Picard was ordered to affix the seals, and all the widow could do was to remove the furnace and the fragments of the glass mask.

The noise of the event soon spread all over Paris. Sainte-Croix was extremely well known, and the, news that he was about to purchase a post in the court had made him known even more widely. Lachaussee was one of the first to learn of his master's death; and hearing that a seal had been set upon his room, he hastened to put in an objection in these terms:

"Objection of Lachaussee, who asserts that for seven years he was in the service of the deceased; that he had given into his charge, two years earlier, 100 pistoles and 200 white crowns, which should be found in a cloth bag under the closet window, and in the same a paper stating that the said sum belonged to him, together with the transfer of 300 livres owed to him by the late M. d'Aubray, councillor; the said transfer made by him at Laserre, together with three receipts from his master of apprenticeship, 100 livres each: these moneys and papers he claims."

To Lachaussee the reply was given that he must wait till the day when the seals were broken, and then if all was as he said, his property would be returned.

But Lachaussee was not the only person who was agitated about the death of Sainte-Croix. The, marquise, who was familiar with all the secrets of this fatal closet, had hurried to the commissary as 2496 soon as she heard of the event, and although it was ten o'clock at night had demanded to speak with him. But he had replied by his head clerk, Pierre Frater, that he was in bed; the marquise insisted, begging them to rouse him up, for she wanted a box that she could not allow to have opened. The clerk then went up to the Sieur Picard's bedroom, but came back saying that what the marquise demanded was for the time being an impossibility, for the commissary was asleep. She saw that it was idle to insist, and went away, saying that she should send a man the next morning to fetch the box. In the morning the man came, offering fifty Louis to the commissary on behalf of the marquise, if he would give her the box. But he replied that the box was in the sealed room, that it would have to be opened, and that if the objects claimed by the marquise were really hers, they would be safely handed over to her. This reply struck the marquise like a thunderbolt. There was no time to be lost: hastily she removed from the rue Neuve-Saint-Paul, where her town house was, to Picpus, her country place. Thence she posted the same evening to Liege, arriving the next morning, and retired to a convent.

The seals had been set on the 31st of July 1672, and they were taken off on the 8th of August following. Just as they set to work a lawyer charged with full powers of acting for the marquise, appeared and put in the following statement: "Alexandre Delamarre, lawyer acting for the Marquise de Brinvilliers, has come forward, and declares that if in the box claimed by his client there is found a promise signed by her for the sum of 30,000 livres, it is a paper taken from her by fraud, against which, in case of her signature being verified, she intends to lodge an appeal for nullification." This formality over, they proceeded to open Sainte-Croix's closet: the key was handed to the commissary Picard by a Carmelite called Friar Victorin. The commissary opened the door, and entered with the parties interested, the officers, and the widow, and they began by setting aside the loose papers, with a view to taking them in order, one at a time. While they were thus busy, a small roll fell down, on which these two words were written: " My Confession." All present, having no reason to suppose Sainte-Croix a bad man, decided that this paper ought not to be read. The deputy for the attorney general on being consulted was of this opinion, and the confession of Sainte-Croix was burnt. This act of conscience performed, they proceeded to make an inventory. One of the first objects that attracted the attention of the officers was the box claimed by Madame de Brinvilliers. Her insistence had provoked curiosity, so they began with it. Everybody went near to see what was in it, and it was opened.

We shall let the report speak: in such cases nothing is so effective or so terrible as the official statement.

"In the closet of Sainte-Croix was found a small box one foot square, on the top of which lay a half-sheet of paper entitled 'My Will,' written on one side and containing these words: 'I humbly entreat any into whose hands this chest may fall to do me the kindness of putting it into the hands of Madame the Marquise de Brinvilliers, resident in the rue Neuve-Saint-Paul, seeing that all the contents concern and belong to her alone, and are of no use to any person in the world apart from herself: in case of her being already dead before me, the box and all its contents should be burnt without opening or disturbing anything. And lest anyone should plead ignorance of the contents, I swear by the God I worship and by all that is most sacred that no untruth is here asserted. If anyone should contravene my wishes that are just and reasonable in this matter, I charge their conscience therewith in discharging my own in this world and the next, protesting that such is my last wish.

"'Given at Paris, the 25th of May after noon, 1672. Signed by Sainte-Croix,'

"And below were written these words: 'There is one packet only addressed to M. Penautier which should be delivered.'"

It may be easily understood that a disclosure of this kind only increased the interest of the scene; there was a murmur of curiosity, and when silence again reigned, the official continued in these words:

"A packet has been found sealed in eight different places with eight different seals. On this is written: 'Papers to be burnt in case of my death, of no consequence to anyone. I humbly beg those into whose hands they may fall to burn them. I give this as a charge upon their conscience; all without opening the packet.' In this packet we find two parcels of sublimate.

"Item, another packet sealed with six different seals, on which is a similar inscription, in which is found more sublimate, half a pound in weight.

"Item, another packet sealed with six different seals, on which is a similar inscription, in which are found three parcels, one containing half an ounce of sublimate, the second 2 1/4 ozs. of Roman vitriol, and the third some calcined prepared vitriol. In the box was found a large square phial, one pint in capacity, full of a clear liquid, which was looked at by M. Moreau, the doctor; he, however, could not tell its nature until it was tested.

"Item, another phial, with half a pint of clear liquid with a white sediment, about which Moreau said the same thing as before.

"Item, a small earthenware pot containing two or three lumps of prepared opium.

"Item, a folded paper containing two drachms of corrosive sublimate powdered.

"Next, a little box containing a sort of stone known as infernal stone.

"Next, a paper containing one ounce of opium.

"Next, a piece of pure antimony weighing three ounces.

"Next, a packet of powder on which was written: 'To check the flow of blood.' Moreau said that it was quince flower and quince buds dried.

"Item, a pack sealed with six seals, on which was written, 'Papers to be burnt in case of death.' In this twenty-four letters were found, said to have been written by the Marquise de Brinvilliers.

"Item, another packet sealed with six seals, on which a similar inscription was written. In this were twenty-seven pieces of paper on each of which was written: 'Sundry curious secrets.'

"Item, another packet with six more seals, on which a similar inscription was written. In this were found seventy-five livres, addressed to different persons. Besides all these, in the box there were two bonds, one from the marquise for 30,000, and one from Penautier for 10,000 francs, their dates corresponding to the time of the deaths of M. d'Aubray and the Sieur de St. Laurent."

The difference in the amount shows that Sainte-Croix had a tariff, and that parricide was more expensive than simple assassination. Thus in his death did Sainte-Croix bequeath the poisons to his mistress and his friend; not content with his own crimes in the past, he wished to be their accomplice in the future.

The first business of the officials was to submit the different substances to analysis, and to experiment with them on animals. The report follows of Guy Simon, an apothecary, who was charged to undertake the analysis and the experiments:

"This artificial poison reveals its nature on examination. It is so disguised that one fails to recognise it, so subtle that it deceives the scientific, so elusive that it escapes the doctor's eye: experiments seem to be at fault with this poison, rules useless, aphorisms ridiculous. The surest experiments are made by the use of the elements or upon animals. In water, ordinary poison falls by its own weight. The water is superior, the poison obeys, falls downwards, and takes the lower place.

"The trial by fire is no less certain: the fire evaporates and disperses all that is innocent and pure, leaving only acrid and sour matter which resists its influence. The effect produced by poisons on animals is still more plain to see: its malignity extends to every part that it reaches, and all that it touches is vitiated; it burns and scorches all the inner parts with a strange, irresistible fire.

"The poison employed by Sainte-Croix has been tried in all the ways, and can defy every experiment. This poison floats in water, it is the superior, and the water obeys it; it escapes in the trial by fire, leaving behind only innocent deposits; in animals it is so skilfully concealed that no one could detect it; all parts of the animal remain healthy and active; even while it is spreading the cause of death, this artificial poison leaves behind the marks and appearance of life. Every sort of experiment has been tried. The first was to pour out several drops of the liquid found into oil of tartar and sea water, and nothing was precipitated into the vessels used; the second was to pour the same liquid into a sanded vessel, and at the bottom there was found nothing acrid or acid to the tongue, scarcely any stains; the third experiment was tried upon an Indian fowl, a pigeon, a dog, and some other animals, which died soon after. When they were opened, however, nothing was found but a little coagulated blood in the ventricle of the heart. Another experiment was giving a white powder to a cat, in a morsel of mutton. The cat vomited for half an hour, and was found dead the next day, but when opened no part of it was found to be affected by the poison. A second trial of the same poison was made upon a pigeon, which soon died. When opened, nothing peculiar was found except a little reddish water in the stomach."

These experiments proved that Sainte-Croix was a learned chemist, and suggested the idea that he did not employ his art for nothing; everybody recalled the sudden, unexpected deaths that had occurred, and the bonds from the marquise and from Penautier looked like blood- money. As one of these two was absent, and the other so powerful and rich that they dared not arrest him without proofs, attention was now paid to the objection put in by Lachaussee.

It was said in the objection that Lachaussee had spent seven years in the service of Sainte-Croix, so he could not have considered the time he had passed with the d'Aubrays as an interruption to this service. The bag containing the thousand pistoles and the three bonds for a hundred livres had been found in the place indicated; thus Lachaussee had a thorough knowledge of this closet: if he knew the closet, he would know about the box; if he knew about the box, he could not be an innocent man. This was enough to induce Madame Mangot de Villarceaux, the lieutenant's widow, to lodge an accusation against him, and in consequence a writ was issued against Lachaussee, and he was arrested.

When this happened, poison was found upon him. The trial came on before the Chatelet. Lachaussee denied his guilt obstinately. The judges thinking they had no sufficient proof, ordered the preparatory question to be applied. Mme. Mangot appealed from a judgment which would probably save the culprit if he had the strength to resist the torture and own to nothing;

[Note: There were two kinds of question, one before and one after the sentence was passed. In the first, an accused person would endure frightful torture in the hope of saving his life, and so would often confess nothing. In the second, there was no hope, and therefore it was not worth while to suffer additional pains.]

so, in virtue of this appeal, a judgment, on March 4th, 1673, declared that Jean Amelin Lachaussee was convicted of having poisoned the lieutenant and the councillor; for which he was to be broken alive on the wheel, having been first subjected to the question both ordinary and extraordinary, with a view to the discovery of his accomplices. At the same time Madame de Brinvilliers was condemned in default of appearance to have her head cut off.

Lachaussee suffered the torture of the boot. This was having each leg fastened between two planks and drawn together in an iron ring, after which wedges were driven in between the middle planks; the ordinary question was with four wedges, the extraordinary with eight. At the third wedge Lachaussee said he was ready to speak; so the question was stopped, and he was carried into the choir of the chapel stretched on a mattress, where, in a weak voice—for he could hardly speak—he begged for half an hour to recover himself. We give a verbatim extract from the report of the question and the execution of the death-sentence:

"Lachaussee, released from the question and laid on the mattress, the official reporter retired. Half an hour later Lachaussee begged that he might return, and said that he was guilty; that Sainte-Croix told him that Madame de Brinvilliers had given him the poison to administer to her brothers; that he had done it in water and soup, had put the reddish water in the lieutenant's glass in Paris, and the clear water in the pie at Villequoy; that Sainte-Croix had promised to keep him always, and to make him a gift of 100 pistolets; that he gave him an account of the effect of the poisons, and that Sainte- Croix had given him some of the waters several times. Sainte-Croix told him that the marquise knew nothing of his other poisonings, but Lachaussee thought she did know, because she had often spoken to him about his poisons; that she wanted to compel him to go away, offering him money if he would go; that she had asked him for the box and its contents; that if Sainte-Croix had been able to put anyone into the service of Madame d'Aubray, the lieutenant's widow, he would possibly have had her poisoned also; for he had a fancy for her daughter."

This declaration, which left no room for doubt, led to the judgment that came next, thus described in the Parliamentary register: "Report of the question and execution on the 24th of March 1673, containing the declarations and confessions of Jean Amelin Lachaussee; the court has ordered that the persons mentioned, Belleguise, Martin, Poitevin, Olivier, Veron pere, the wife of Quesdon the wigmaker, be summoned to appear before the court to be interrogated and heard concerning matters arising from the present inquiry, and orders that the decree of arrest against Lapierre and summons against Penautier decreed by the criminal lieutenant shall be carried out. In Parliament, 27th March 1673." In virtue of this judgment, Penautier, Martin, and Belleguise were interrogated on the 2lst, 22nd, and 24th of April. On the 26th of July, Penautier was discharged; fuller information was desired concerning Belleguise, and the arrest of Martin was ordered. On the 24th of March, Lachaussee had been broken on the wheel. As to Exili, the beginner of it all, he had disappeared like Mephistopheles after Faust's end, and nothing was heard of him. Towards the end of the year Martin was released for want of sufficient evidence. But the Marquise de Brinvilliers remained at

Liege, and although she was shut up in a convent she had by no means abandoned one, at any rate, of the most worldly pleasures. She had soon found consolation for the death of Sainte-Croix, whom, all the same, she had loved so much as to be willing to kill herself for his sake. But she had adopted a new lover, Theria by name. About this man it has been impossible to get any information, except that his name was several times mentioned during the trial. Thus, all the accusations had, one by one, fallen upon her, and it was resolved to seek her out in the retreat where she was supposed to be safe. The mission was difficult and very delicate. Desgrais, one of the cleverest of the officials, offered to undertake it. He was a handsome man, thirty-six years old or thereabouts: nothing in his looks betrayed his connection with the police; he wore any kind of dress with equal ease and grace, and was familiar with every grade in the social scale, disguising himself as a wretched tramp or a noble lord. He was just the right man, so his offer was accepted.

He started accordingly for Liege, escorted by several archers, and, fortified by a letter from the king addressed to the Sixty of that town, wherein Louis xiv demanded the guilty woman to be given up for punishment. After examining the letter, which Desgrais had taken pains to procure, the council authorised the extradition of the marquise.

This was much, but it was not all. The marquise, as we know, had taken refuge in a convent, where Desgrais dared not arrest her by force, for two reasons: first, because she might get information beforehand, and hide herself in one of the cloister retreats whose secret is known only to the superior; secondly, because Liege was so religious a town that the event would produce a great sensation: the act might be looked upon as a sacrilege, and might bring about a popular rising, during which the marquise might possibly contrive to escape. So Desgrais paid a visit to his wardrobe, and feeling that an abbe's dress would best free him from suspicion, he appeared at the doors of the convent in the guise of a fellow-countryman just returned from Rome, unwilling to pass through Liege without presenting his compliments to the lovely and unfortunate marquise. Desgrais had just the manner of the younger son of a great house: he

26

was as flattering as a courtier, as enterprising as a musketeer. In this first visit he made himself attractive by his wit and his audacity, so much so that more easily than he had dared to hope, he got leave to pay a second call. The second visit was not long delayed: Desgrais presented himself the very next day. Such eagerness was flattering to the marquise, so Desgrais was received even better than the night before. She, a woman of rank and fashion, for more than a year had been robbed of all intercourse with people of a certain set, so with Desgrais the marquise resumed her Parisian manner. Unhappily the charming abbe was to leave Liege in a few days; and on that account he became all the more pressing, and a third visit, to take place next day, was formally arranged. Desgrais was punctual: the marquise was impatiently waiting him; but by a conjunction of circumstances that Desgrais had no doubt arranged beforehand, the amorous meeting was disturbed two or three times just as they were getting more intimate and least wanting to be observed. Desgrais complained of these tiresome checks; besides, the marquise and he too would be compromised: he owed concealment to his cloth: He begged her to grant him a rendezvous outside the town, in some deserted walk, where there would be no fear of their being recognised or followed: the marquise hesitated no longer than would serve to put a price on the favour she was granting, and the rendezvous was fixed for the same evening.

The evening came: both waited with the same impatience, but with very different hopes. The marquise found Desgrais at the appointed spot: he gave her his arm then holding her hand in his own, he gave a sign, the archers appeared, the lover threw off his mask, Desgrais was confessed, and the marquise was his prisoner. Desgrais left her in the hands of his men, and hastily made his way to the convent. Then, and not before, he produced his order from the Sixty, by means of which he opened the marquise's room. Under her bed he found a box, which he seized and sealed; then he went back to her, and gave the order to start.

When the marquise saw the box in the hands of Desgrais, she at first appeared stunned; quickly recovering, she claimed a paper inside it which contained her confession. Desgrais refused, and as he turned round for the carriage to come forward, she tried to choke herself by swallowing a pin. One of the archers, called Claude, Rolla, perceiving her intention, contrived to get the pin out of her mouth. After this, Desgrais commanded that she should be doubly watched.

They stopped for supper. An archer called Antoine Barbier was present at the meal, and watched so that no knife or fork should be put on the table, or any instrument with which she could wound or kill herself. The marquise, as she put her glass to her mouth as though to drink, broke a little bit off with her teeth; but the archer saw it in time, and forced her to put it out on her plate. Then she promised him, if he would save her, that she would make his fortune. He asked what he would have to do for that. She proposed that he should cut Desgrais' throat; but he refused, saying that he was at her service in any other way. So she asked him for pen and paper, and wrote this letter:

"DEAR THERIA,—I am in the hands of Desgrais, who is taking me by road from Liege to Paris. Come quickly and save me."

Antoine Barbier took the letter, promising to deliver it at the right address; but he gave it to Desgrais instead. The next day, finding that this letter had not been pressing enough, she wrote him another, saying that the escort was only eight men, who could be easily overcome by four or five determined assailants, and she counted on him to strike this bald stroke. But, uneasy when she got no answer and no result from her letters, she despatched a third missive to Theria. In this she implored him by his own salvation, if he were not strong enough to attack her escort and save her, at least to kill two of the four horses by which she was conveyed, and to profit by the moment of confusion to seize the chest and throw it into the fire; otherwise, she declared, she was lost. Though Theria received none of these letters, which were one by one handed over by Barbier to Desgrais, he all the same did go to Maestricht, where the marquise was to pass, of his own accord. There he tried to bribe the archers, offering much as 10,000 livres, but they were incorruptible. At Rocroy the cortege met M. Palluau, the councillor, whom the Parliament had sent after the prisoner, that he might put questions to her at a time when she least expected them, and so would not have prepared her answers. Desgrais told him all that had passed, and specially called his attention to the famous box, the object of so much anxiety and so many eager instructions. M. de Palluau opened it, and found among other things a paper headed " My Confession." This confession was a proof that the guilty feel great need of discovering their crimes either to mankind or to a merciful God. Sainte-Croix, we know, had made a confession that was burnt, and here was the marquise equally imprudent. The confession contained seven articles, and began thus, "I confess to God, and to you, my father," and was a complete avowal, of all the crimes she had committed.

In the first article she accused herself of incendiarism ;

In the second, of having ceased to be a virgin at seven years of age;

In the third of having poisoned her father;

In the fourth, of having poisoned her two brothers;

In the fifth, that she had tried to poison her sister, a Carmelite nun.

The two other articles were concerned with the description of strange and unnatural sins. In this woman there was something of Locusta and something of Messalina as well: antiquity could go no further.

M. de Palluau, fortified by his knowledge of this important document, began his examination forthwith. We give it verbatim, rejoicing that we may substitute an official report for our own narrative.

Asked why she fled to Liege, she replied that she left France on account of some business with her sister-in-law.

Asked if she had any knowledge of the papers found in the box, she replied that in the box there were several family papers, and among them a general confession which she desired to make; when she wrote it, however, her mind was disordered; she knew not what she had said or done, being distraught at the time, in a foreign country, deserted by her relatives, forced to borrow every penny.

Asked as to the first article, what house it was she had burnt, she replied that she had not burnt anything, but when she wrote that she was out of her senses.

Asked about the six other articles she replied that she had no recollection of them.

Asked if she had not poisoned her father and brothers, she replied that she knew nothing at all about it.

Asked if it were not Lachaussee who poisoned her brothers, she replied that she knew nothing about it.

Asked if she did not know that her sister could not live long, having been poisoned, she said that she expected her sister to die, because she suffered in the same way as her brothers; that she had lost all memory of the time when she wrote this confession; admitted that she left France by the advice of her relations.

Asked why her relations had advised her thus, she replied that it was in connection with her brothers' affairs; admitted seeing Sainte-Croix since his release from the Bastille.

Asked if Sainte-Croix had not persuaded her to get rid of her father, she replied that she could not remember; neither did she remember if Sainte-Croix had given her powders or other drugs, nor if Sainte-Croix had told her he knew how to make her rich.

Eight letters having been produced, asked to whom she had written them, she replied that she did not remember.

Asked why she had promised to pay 30,000 livres to Sainte-Croix, she replied that she intended to entrust this sum to his care, so that she might make use of it when she wanted it, believing him to be her friend; she had not wished this to be known, by reason of her creditors; that she had an acknowledgment from Sainte-Croix, but had lost it in her travels; that her husband knew nothing about it.

Asked if the promise was made before or after the death of her brothers, she replied that she could not remember, and it made no difference.

Asked if she knew an apothecary called Glazer, she replied that she had consulted him three times about inflammation.

Asked why she wrote to Theria to get hold of the box, she replied that she did not understand.

Asked why, in writing to Theria, she had said she was lost unless he got hold of the box, she replied that she could not remember.

Asked if she had seen during the journey with her father the first symptoms of his malady, she replied that she had not noticed that her father was ill on the journey, either going or coming back in 1666.

Asked if she had not done business with Penautier, she replied that Penautier owed her 30,000 livres.

Asked how this was, she replied that she and her husband had lent Penautier 10,000 crowns, that he had paid it back, and since then they had had no dealings with him.

The marquise took refuge, we see, in a complete system of denial: arrived in Paris, and confined in the Conciergerie, she did the same; but soon other terrible charges were added, which still further overwhelmed her.

The sergeant Cluet deposed: that, observing a lackey to M. d'Aubray, the councillor, to be the man Lachaussee, whom he had seen in the service of Sainte-Croix, he said to the marquise that if her brother knew that Lachaussee had been with Sainte-Croix he would not like it, but that Madame de Brinvilliers exclaimed, "Dear me, don't tell my brothers; they would give him a thrashing, no doubt, and he may just as well get his wages as any body else." He said nothing to the d'Aubrays, though he saw Lachaussee paying daily visits to Sainte-Croix and to the marquise, who was worrying Sainte-Croix to let her have her box, and wanted her bill for two or three thousand pistoles. Other wise she would have had him assassinated. She often said that she was very anxious that no one should see the contents of the box; that it was a very important matter, but only concerned herself. After the box was opened, the witness added, he had told the marquise, that the commissary Picard said to Lachaussee that there were strange things in it; but the lady blushed, and changed the subject. He asked her if she were not an accomplice. She said, "What! I?" but then muttered to herself: " Lachaussee ought to be sent off to Picardy." The witness repeated that she had been after Sainte-Croix along time about the box, and if she had got it she would have had his throat cut. The witness further said that when he told Briancourt that Lachaussee was taken and would doubtless confess all, Briancourt, speaking of the marquise, remarked, "She is a lost woman." That d'Aubray's daughter had called Briancourt a rogue, but Briancourt had replied that she little knew what obligations she was under to him; that they had wanted to poison both her and the lieutenant's widow, and he alone had hindered it. He had heard from Briancourt that the marquise had often said that there are means to get rid of people one dislikes, and they can easily be put an end to in a bowl of soup.

The girl Edme Huet, a woman of Brescia, deposed that Sainte-Croix went to see the marquise every day, and that in a box belonging to that lady she had seen two little packets containing sublimate in powder and in paste: she recognised these, because she was an apothecary's daughter. She added that one day Madame de Brinvilliers, after a dinner party, in a merry mood, said, showing her a little box, "Here is vengeance on one's enemies: this box is small, but holds plenty of successsions!" That she gave back the box into her hands, but soon changing from her sprightly mood, she cried, "Good heavens, what have I said? Tell nobody." That Lambert, clerk at the palace, told her he had brought the packets to Madame from Sainte-Croix; that Lachaussee often went to see her; and that she herself, not being paid ten pistoles which the marquise owed her, went to complain to Sainte-Croix, threatening to tell the lieutenant what she had seen; and accordingly the ten pistoles were paid; further, that the marquise and Sainte-Croix always kept poison about them, to make use of, in case of being arrested.

Laurent Perrette, living with Glazer, said that he had often seen a lady call on his mistress with Sainte-Croix; that the footman told him she was the Marquise de Brinvilliers; that he would wager his head on it that they came to Glazer's to make poison; that when they came they used to leave their carriage at the Foire Saint-Germain.

Marie de Villeray, maid to the marquise, deposed that after the death of M. d'Aubray the councillor, Lachaussee came to see the lady and spoke with her in private; that Briancourt said she had caused the death of a worthy men; that Briancourt every day took some electuary for fear of being poisoned, and it was no doubt due to this precaution that he was still alive; but he feared he would be stabbed, because she had told him the secret about the poisoning; that d'Aubray's daughter had to be warned; and that there was a similar design against the tutor of M. de Brinvillier's children. Marie de Villeray added that two days after the death of the councillor, when Lachaussee was in Madame's bedroom, Couste, the late lieutenant's secretary, was announced, and Lachaussee had to be hidden in the alcove by the bed. Lachaussee brought the marquise a letter from Sainte-Croix.

Francois Desgrais, officer, deposed that when he was given the king's orders he arrested the marquise at Liege; that he found under her bed a box which he sealed; that the lady had demanded a paper which was in it, containing her confession, but he refused it; that on the road to Paris the marquise had told him that she believed it was Glazer who made the poisons for Sainte-Croix; that Sainte-Croix, who had made a rendezvous with her one day at the cross Saint-Honore, there showed her four little bottles, saying, "See what Glazer has sent me." She asked him for one, but Sainte-Croix said he would rather die than give it up. He added that the archer Antoine Barbier had given him three letters written by the marquise to

Theria; that in the first she had told him to come at once and snatch her from the hands of the soldiers; that in the second she said that the escort was only composed of eight persons, who could he worsted by five men; that in the third she said that if he could not save her from the men who were taking her away, he should at least approach the commissary, and killing his valet's horse and two other horses in his carriage, then take the box, and burn it; otherwise she was lost.

Laviolette, an archer, deposed that on the evening of the arrest. the marquise had a long pin and tried to put it in her mouth; that he stopped her, and told her that she was very wicked; that he perceived that people said the truth and that she had poisoned all her family; to which she replied, that if she had, it was only through following bad advice, and that one could not always be good.

Antoine Barbier, an archer, said that the marquise at table took up a glass as though to drink, and tried to swallow a piece of it; that he prevented this, and she promised to make his fortune if only he would save her; that she wrote several letters to Theria; that during the whole journey she tried all she could to swallow pins, bits of glass, and earth; that she had proposed that he should cut Desgrais' throat, and kill the commissary's valet; that she had bidden him get the box and burn it, and bring a lighted torch to burn everything; that she had written to Penautier from the Conciergerie; that she gave him, the letter, and he pretended to deliver it.

Finally, Francoise Roussel deposed that she had been in the service of the marquise, and the lady had one day given her some preserved gooseberries; that she had eaten some on the point of her knife, and at once felt ill. She also gave her a slice of mutton, rather wet, which she ate, afterwards suffering great pain in the stomach, feeling as though she had been pricked in the heart, and for three years had felt the same, believing herself poisoned.

It was difficult to continue a system of absolute denial in face of proofs like these. The marquise persisted, all the same, that she was in no way guilty; and Maitre Nivelle, one of the best lawyers of the period, consented to defend her cause.

He combated one charge after another, in a remarkably clever way, owning to the adulterous connection of the marquise with Sainte-Croix, but denying her participation in the murders of the d'Aubrays, father and sons: these he ascribed entirely to the vengeance desired by Sainte-Croix. As to the confession, the strongest and, he maintained, the only evidence against Madame de Brinvilliers, he attacked its validity by bringing forward certain similar cases, where the evidence supplied by the accused against themselves had not been admitted by reason of the legal action: 'Non auditur perire volens'. He cited three instances, and as they are themselves interesting, we copy them verbatim from his notes.

FIRST CASE

Dominicus Soto, a very famous canonist and theologian, confessor to Charles V, present at the first meetings of the Council of Trent under Paul III, propounds a question about a man who had lost a paper on which he had written down his sins. It happened that this paper fell into the hands of an ecclesiastical judge, who wished to put in information against the writer on the strength of this document. Now this judge was justly punished by his superior, because confession is so sacred that even that which is destined to constitute the confession should be wrapped in eternal silence. In accordance with this precedent, the following judgment, reported in the 'Traite des Confesseurs', was given by Roderic Acugno. A Catalonian, native of Barcelona, who was condemned to death for homicide and owned his guilt, refused to confess when the hour of punishment arrived. However strongly pressed, he resisted, and so violently, giving no reason, that all were persuaded that his mind was unhinged by the fear of death. Saint-Thomas of Villeneuve, Archbishop of Valencia, heard of his obstinacy. Valencia was the place where his sentence was given. The worthy prelate was so charitable as to try to persuade the criminal to make his confession, so as not to lose his soul as well as his body. Great was his surprise, when he asked the reason of the refusal, to hear the doomed man declare that he hated confessors, because he had been condemned through the treachery of his own priest, who was the only person who knew about the murder. In confession he had admitted his crime and said where the body was buried, and all about it; his confessor had revealed it all, and he could not deny it, and so he had been condemned. He had only just learned, what he did not know at the time he confessed, that his confessor was the brother of the man he had killed, and that the desire for vengeance had prompted the bad priest to betray his confession. Saint-Thomas, hearing this, thought that this incident was of more importance than the trial, which concerned the life of only one person, whereas the honour of religion was at stake, with consequences infinitely more important. He felt he must verify this statement, and summoned the confessor. When he had admitted the breach of faith, the judges were obliged to revoke their sentence and pardon the criminal, much to the gratification of the public mind. The confessor was adjudged a very severe penance, which Saint-Thomas modified because of his prompt avowal of his fault, and still more because he had given an opportunity for the public exhibition of that reverence which judges themselves are bound to pay to confessions.

SECOND CASE

In 1579 an innkeeper at Toulouse killed with his own hand, unknown to the inmates of his house, a stranger who had come to lodge with him, and buried him secretly in the cellar. The wretch then suffered from remorse, and confessed the crime with all its circumstances, telling his confessor where the body was buried. The relations of the dead man, after making all possible search to get news of him, at last proclaimed through the town a large reward to be given to anyone who would discover what had happened to him. The confessor, tempted by this bait, secretly gave word that they had only to search in the innkeeper's cellar and they would find the corpse. And they found it in the place indicated. The innkeeper was thrown into prison, was tortured, and confessed his crime. But afterwards he always maintained that his confessor was the only person who could have betrayed him. Then the Parliament, indignant with such means of finding out the truth, declared him innocent, failing other proof than what came through his confessor. The confessor was himself condemned to be hanged, and his body was burnt. So fully did the tribunal in its wisdom recognise the importance of securing the sanctity of a sacrament that is indispensable to salvation.

THIRD CASE

An Armenian woman had inspired a violent passion in a young Turkish gentleman, but her prudence was long an obstacle to her lover's desires. At last he went beyond all bounds, and threatened to kill both her and her husband if she refused to gratify him. Frightened by this threat, which she knew too well he would carry out, she feigned consent, and gave the Turk a rendezvous at her house at an hour when she said her husband would be absent; but by arrangement the husband arrived, and although the Turk was armed with a sabre and a pair of pistols, it so befell that they were fortunate enough to kill their enemy, whom they buried under their dwelling unknown to all the world. But some days after the event they went to confess to a priest of their nation, and revealed every detail of the tragic story. This unworthy minister of the Lord supposed that in a Mahommedan country, where the laws of the priesthood and the functions of a confessor are either unknown or disapproved, no examination would be made into the source of his information, and that his evidence would have the same weight as any other accuser's. So he resolved to make a profit and gratify his own avarice. Several times he visited the husband and wife, always borrowing considerable sums, and threatening to reveal their crime if they refused him. The first few times the poor creatures gave in to his exactions; but the moment came at last when, robbed of all their fortune, they were obliged to refuse the sum he demanded. Faithful to his threat, the priest, with a view to more reward, at once denounced them to the dead man's father. He, who had adored his son, went to the vizier, told him he had identified the murderers through their confessor, and asked for justice. But this denunciation had by no means the desired effect. The vizier, on the contrary, felt deep pity for the wretched Armenians, and indignation against the priest who had betrayed them. He put the accuser into a room which adjoined the court, and sent for the Armenian bishop to ask what confession really was, and what punishment was deserved by a priest who betrayed it, and what was the fate of those whose crimes were made known in this fashion. The bishop replied that the secrets of confession are inviolable, that Christians burn the priest who reveals them, and absolve those whom he accuses, because the avowal made by the guilty to the priest is proscribed by the Christian religion, on pain of eternal damnation. The vizier, satisfied with the answer, took the bishop into another room, and summoned the accused to declare all the circumstances: the poor wretches, half dead, fell at the vizier's feet. The woman spoke, explaining that the necessity of defending life and honour had driven them to take up arms to kill their enemy. She added that God alone had witnessed their crime, and it would still be unknown had not the law of the same God compelled them to confide it to the ear of one of His ministers for their forgiveness. Now the priest's insatiable avarice had ruined them first and then denounced them. The vizier made them go into a third room, and ordered the treacherous priest to be confronted with the bishop, making him again rehearse the penalties incurred by those who betray confessions. Then, applying this to the guilty priest, he condemned him to be burnt alive in a public place;—in anticipation, said he, of burning in hell, where he would assuredly receive the punishment of his infidelity and crimes. The sentence was executed without delay.

In spite of the effect which the advocate intended to produce by these three cases, either the judges rejected them, or perhaps they thought the other evidence without the confession was enough, and it was soon clear to everyone, by the way the trial went forward, that the marquise would be condemned. Indeed, before sentence was pronounced, on the morning of July 16th, 1676, she saw M. Pirot, doctor of the Sorbonne, come into her prison, sent by the chief president. This worthy magistrate, foreseeing the issue, and feeling that one so guilty should not be left till the last moment, had sent the good priest. The latter, although he had objected that the Conciergerie had its own two chaplains, and added that he was too feeble to undertake such a task, being unable even to see another man bled without feeling ill, accepted the painful mission, the president having so strongly urged it, on the ground that in this case he needed a man who could be entirely trusted. The president, in fact, declared that, accustomed as he was to dealing with criminals, the strength of the marquise amazed him. The day before he summoned M. Pirot, he had worked at the trial from morning to night, and for thirteen hours the accused had been confronted with Briancourt, one of the chief witnesses against her. On that very ,day, there had been five hours more, and she had borne it all, showing as much respect towards her judges as haughtiness towards the witness, reproaching him as a miserable valet, given to drink, and protesting that as he had been dismissed for his misdemeanours, his testimony against her ought to go for nothing. So the chief president felt no hope of breaking her inflexible spirit, except by the agency of a minister of religion; for it was not enough to put her to death, the poisons must perish with her, or else society would gain nothing. The doctor Pirot came to the marquise with a letter from her sister, who, as we know, was a nun bearing the name of Sister Marie at the convent Saint-Jacques. Her letter exhorted the marquise, in the most touching and affectionate terms, to place her confidence in the good priest, and look upon him not only as a helper but as a friend.

When M. Pirot came before the marquise, she had just left the dock, where she had been for three hours without confessing anything, or seeming in the least touched by what the president said, though he, after acting the part of judge, addressed her simply as a Christian, and showing her what her deplorable position was, appearing now for the last time before men, and destined so soon to appear before God, spoke to her such moving words that he broke down himself, and the oldest and most obdurate judges present wept when they heard him. When the marquise perceived the doctor, suspecting that her trial was leading her to death, she approached him, saying:

"You have come, sir, because — —"

But Father Chavigny, who was with M. Pirot; interrupted her, saying:

"Madame, we will begin with a prayer."

They all fell on their knees invoking the Holy Spirit; then the marquise asked them to add a prayer to the Virgin, and, this prayer finished, she went up to the doctor, and, beginning afresh, said:

"Sir, no doubt the president has sent you to give me consolation: with you I am to pass the little life I have left. I have long been eager to see you."

"Madame," the doctor replied, "I come to render you any spiritual office that I can; I only wish it were on another occasion."

"We must have resolution, sir," said she, smiling, "for all things."

Then turning to Father Chavigny, she said:

"My father, I am very grateful to you for bringing the doctor here, and for all the other visits you have been willing to pay me. Pray to God for me, I entreat you; henceforth I shall speak with no one but the doctor, for with him I must speak of things that can only be discussed tete-a-tete. Farewell, then, my father; God will reward you for the attention you have been willing to bestow upon me."

With these words the father retired, leaving the marquise alone with the doctor and the two men and one woman always in attendance on her. They were in a large room in the Montgomery tower extending, throughout its whole length. There was at the end of the room a bed with grey curtains for the lady, and a folding-bed for the custodian. It is said to have been the same room where the poet Theophile was once shut up, and near the door there were still verses in his well-known style written by his hand.

As soon as the two men and the woman saw for what the doctor had come, they retired to the end of the room, leaving the marquise free to ask for and receive the consolations brought her by the man of God. Then the two sat at a table side by side. The marquise thought she was already condemned, and began to speak on that assumption; but the doctor told her that sentence was not yet given, and he did not know precisely when it would be, still less what it would be; but at these words the marquise interrupted him.

"Sir," she said, "I am not troubled about the future. If my sentence is not given yet, it soon will be. I expect the news this morning, and I know it will be death: the only grace I look for from the president is a delay between the sentence and its execution; for if I were executed to-day I should have very little time to prepare, and I feel I have need for more."

The doctor did not expect such words, so he was overjoyed to learn what she felt. In addition to what the president had said, he had heard from Father Chavigny that he had told her the Sunday before that it was very unlikely she would escape death, and indeed, so far as one could judge by reports in the town, it was a foregone conclusion. When he said so, at first she had appeared stunned, and said with an air of great terror, "Father, must I die?" And when he tried to speak words of consolation, she had risen and shaken her head, proudly replying—

"No, no, father; there is no need to encourage me. I will play my part, and that at once: I shall know how to die like a woman of spirit."

Then the father had told her that we cannot prepare for death so quickly and so easily; and that we have to be in readiness for a long time, not to be taken by surprise; and she had replied that she needed but a quarter of an hour to confess in, and one moment to die.

So the doctor was very glad to find that between Sunday and Thursday her feelings had changed so much.

"Yes," said she, "the more I reflect the more I feel that one day would not be enough to prepare myself for God's tribunal, to be judged by Him after men have judged me."

"Madame," replied the doctor, "I do not know what or when your sentence will be; but should it be death, and given to-day, I may venture to promise you that it will not be carried out before to-morrow. But although death is as yet uncertain, I think it well that you should be prepared for any event."

"Oh, my death is quite certain," said she, "and I must not give way to useless hopes. I must repose in you the great secrets of my whole life; but, father, before this opening of my heart, let me hear from your lips the opinion you have formed of me, and what you think in my present state I ought to do."

"You perceive my plan," said the doctor, "and you anticipate what I was about to say. Before entering into the secrets of your conscience, before opening the discussion of your affairs with God, I am ready, madame, to give you certain definite rules. I do not yet know whether you are guilty at all, and I suspend my judgment as to all the crimes you are accused of, since of them I can learn nothing except through your confession. Thus it is my duty still to doubt your guilt. But I cannot be ignorant of what you are accused of: this is a public matter, and has reached my ears; for, as you may imagine, madame, your affairs have made a great stir, and there are few people who know nothing about them."

"Yes," she said, smiling, "I know there has been a great deal of talk, and I am in every man's mouth."

"Then," replied the doctor, "the crime you are accused of is poisoning. If you are guilty, as is believed, you cannot hope that God will pardon you unless you make known to your judges what the poison is, what is its composition and what its antidote, also the names of your accomplices. Madame, we must lay hands on all these evil-doers without exception; for if you spared them, they would be able to make use of your poison, and you would then be guilty of all the murders committed by them after your death, because you did not give them over to the judges during your life; thus one might say you survive yourself, for your crime survives you. You know, madame, that a sin in the moment of death is never pardoned, and that to get remission for your crimes, if crimes you have, they must die when you die: for if you slay them not, be very sure they will slay you."

"Yes, I am sure of that," replied the marquise, after a moment of silent thought; "and though I will not admit that I am guilty, I promise, if I am guilty, to weigh your words. But one question, sir, and pray take heed that an answer is necessary. Is there not crime in this world that is beyond pardon? Are not some people guilty of sins so terrible and so numerous that the Church dares not pardon them, and if God, in His justice, takes account of them, He cannot for all His mercy pardon them? See, I begin with this question, because, if I am to have no hope, it is needless for me to confess."

"I wish to think, madame," replied the doctor, in spite of himself half frightened at the marquise, "that this your first question is only put by way of a general thesis, and has nothing to do with your own state. I shall answer the question without any personal application. No, madame, in this life there are no unpardonable sinners, terrible and numerous howsoever their sins may be. This is an article of faith, and without holding it you could not die a good Catholic. Some doctors, it is true, have before now maintained the contrary, but they have been condemned as heretics. Only despair and final impenitence are unpardonable, and they are not sins of our life but in our death."

"Sir," replied the marquise, "God has given me grace to be convinced by what you say, and I believe He will pardon all sins— that He has often exercised this power. Now all my trouble is that He may not deign to grant all His goodness to one so wretched as I am, a creature so unworthy of the favours already bestowed on her."

The doctor reassured her as best he could, and began to examine her attentively as they conversed together. "She was," he said, "a woman naturally courageous and fearless; naturally gentle and good; not easily excited; clever and penetrating, seeing things very clearly in her mind, and expressing herself well and in few but careful words; easily finding a way out of a difficulty, and choosing her line of conduct in the most embarrassing circumstances; light-minded and fickle; unstable, paying no attention if the same thing were said several times over. For this reason," continued the doctor, "I was obliged to alter what I had to say from time to time, keeping her but a short time to one subject, to which, however, I would return later, giving the matter a new appearance and disguising it a little. She spoke little and well, with no sign of learning and no affectation, always, mistress of herself, always composed and saying just what she intended to say. No one would have supposed from her face or from her conversation that she was so wicked as she must have been, judging by her public avowal of the parricide. It is surprising, therefore—and one must bow down before the judgment of God when He leaves mankind to himself—that a mind evidently of some grandeur, professing fearlessness in the most untoward and unexpected events, an immovable firmness and a resolution to await and to endure death if so it must be, should yet be so criminal as she was proved to be by the parricide to which she confessed before her judges. She had nothing in her face that would indicate such evil. She had very abundant chestnut hair, a rounded, well-shaped face, blue eyes very pretty and gentle, extraordinarily white skin, good nose, and no disagreeable feature. Still, there was nothing unusually attractive in the face: already she was a little wrinkled, and looked older than her age. Something made me ask at our first interview how old she was. 'Monsieur,' she said, 'if I were to live till Sainte-Madeleine's day I should be forty-six. On her day I came into the world, and I bear her name. I was christened Marie-Madeleine. But near to the day as we now are, I shall not live so long: I must end to-day, or at latest to-morrow, and it will be a favour to give me the one day. For this kindness I rely on your word.' Anyone would have thought she was quite forty-eight. Though her face as a rule looked so gentle, whenever an unhappy thought crossed her mind she showed it by a contortion that frightened one at first, and from time to time I saw her face twitching with anger, scorn, or ill-will. I forgot to say that she was very little and thin. Such is, roughly given, a description of her body and mind, which I very soon came to know, taking pains from the first to observe her, so as to lose no time in acting on what I discovered."

As she was giving a first brief sketch of her life to her confessor, the marquise remembered that he had not yet said mass, and reminded him herself that it was time to do so, pointing out to him the chapel of the Conciergerie. She begged him to say a mass for her and in honour of Our Lady, so that she might gain the intercession of the Virgin at the throne of God. The Virgin she had always taken for her patron saint, and in the midst of her crimes and disorderly life had never ceased in her peculiar devotion. As she could not go with the priest, she promised to be with him at least in the spirit. He left her at half-past ten in the morning, and after four hours spent alone together, she had been induced by his piety and gentleness to make confessions that could not be wrung from her by the threats of the judges or the fear of the question. The holy and devout priest said his mass, praying the Lord's help for confessor and penitent alike. After mass, as he returned, he learned from a librarian called Seney, at the porter's lodge, as he was taking a glass of wine, that judgment had been given, and that Madame de Brinvilliers was to have her hand cut off. This severity—as a fact, there was a mitigation of the sentence—made him feel yet more interest in his penitent, and he hastened back to her side.

As soon as she saw the door open, she advanced calmly towards him, and asked if he had truly prayed for her; and when he assured her of this, she said, "Father, shall I have the consolation of receiving the viaticum before I die?"

"Madame," replied the doctor, "if you are condemned to death, you must die without that sacrament, and I should be deceiving you if I let you hope for it. We have heard of the death of the constable of Saint-Paul without his obtaining this grace, in spite of all his entreaties. He was executed in sight of the towers of Notre-Dame. He offered his own prayer, as you may offer yours, if you suffer the same fate. But that is all: God, in His goodness, allows it to suffice."

"But," replied the marquise, "I believe M. de Cinq-Mars and M. de Thou communicated before their death."

"I think not, madame," said the doctor; " for it is not so said in the pages of Montresor or any other book that describes their execution."

"But M. de Montmorency?" said she.

"But M. de Marillac?" replied the doctor.

In truth, if the favour had been granted to the first, it had been refused to the second, and the marquise was specially struck thereby, for M. de Marillac was of her own family, and she was very proud of the connection. No doubt she was unaware that M. de Rohan had received the sacrament at the midnight mass said for the salvation of his soul by Father Bourdaloue, for she said nothing about it, and hearing the doctor's answer, only sighed.

"Besides," he continued, "in recalling examples of the kind, madame, you must not build upon them, please: they are extraordinary cases, not the rule. You must expect no privilege; in your case the ordinary laws will be carried out, and your fate will not differ from the fate of other condemned persons. How would it have been had you lived and died before the reign of Charles VI? Up to the reign of this prince, the guilty died without confession, and it was only by this king's orders that there was a relaxation of this severity. Besides, communion is not absolutely necessary to salvation, and one may communicate spiritually in reading the word, which is like the body; in uniting oneself with the Church, which is the mystical substance of Christ; and in suffering for Him and with Him, this last communion of agony that is your portion, madame, and is the most perfect communion of all. If you heartily detest your crime and love God with all your soul, if you have faith and charity, your death is a martyrdom and a new baptism."

"Alas, my God," replied the marquise, "after what you tell me, now that I know the executioner's hand was necessary to my salvation, what should I have become had I died at Liege? Where should I have been now? And even if I had not been taken, and had lived another twenty years away from France, what would my death have been, since it needed the scaffold for my purification? Now I see all my wrong-doings, and the worst of all is the last—I mean my effrontery before the judges. But all is not yet lost, God be thanked; and as I have one last examination to go through, I desire to make a complete confession about my whole life. You, Sir, I entreat specially to ask pardon on my behalf of the first president; yesterday, when I was in the dock, he spoke very touching words to me, and I was deeply moved; but I would not show it, thinking that if I made no avowal the evidence would not be sufficiently strong to convict me. But it has happened otherwise, and I must have scandalised my judges by such an exhibition of hardihood. Now I recognise my fault, and will repair it. Furthermore, sir, far from feeling angry with the president for the judgment he to-day passes against me, far from complaining of the prosecutor who has demanded it, I thank them both most humbly, for my salvation depends upon it."

The doctor was about to answer, encouraging her, when the door opened: it was dinner coming in, for it was now half-past one. The marquise paused and watched what was brought in, as though she were playing hostess in her own country house. She made the woman and the two men who watched her sit down to the table, and turning to the doctor, said, "Sir, you will not wish me to stand on ceremony with you; these good people always dine with me to keep me company, and if you approve, we will do the same to-day. This is the last meal," she added, addressing them, "that I shall take with you." Then turning to the woman, "Poor Madame du Rus," said she, "I have been a trouble to you for a long time; but have a little patience, and you will soon be rid of me. To-morrow you can go to Dravet; you will have time, for in seven or eight hours from now there will be nothing more to do for me, and I shall be in the gentleman's hands; you will not be allowed near me. After then, you can go away for good; for I don't suppose you will have the heart to see me executed." All this she said quite calmly, but not with pride. From time to time her people tried to hide their tears, and she made a sign of pitying them. Seeing that the dinner was on the table and nobody eating, she invited the doctor to take some soup, asking him to excuse the cabbage in it, which made it a common soup and unworthy of his acceptance. She herself took some soup and two eggs, begging her fellow-guests to excuse her for not serving them, pointing out that no knife or fork had been set in her place.

When the meal was almost half finished, she begged the doctor to let her drink his health. He replied by drinking hers, and she seemed to be quite charmed by, his condescension. "To-morrow is a fast day," said she, setting down her glass, "and although it will be a day of great fatigue for me, as I shall have to undergo the question as well as death, I intend to obey the orders of the Church and keep my fast."

"Madame," replied the doctor, "if you needed soup to keep you up, you would not have to feel any scruple, for it will be no self-indulgence, but a necessity, and the Church does not exact fasting in such a case."

"Sir," replied the marquise, "I will make no difficulty about it, if it is necessary and if you order it; but it will not be needed, I think: if I have some soup this evening for supper, and some more made stronger than usual a little before midnight, it will be enough to last me through to-morrow, if I have two fresh eggs to take after the question."

"In truth," says the priest in the account we give here, "I was alarmed by this calm behaviour. I trembled when I heard her give orders to the concierge that the soup was to be made stronger than usual and that she was to have two cups before midnight. When dinner was over, she was given pen and ink, which she had already asked for, and told me that she had a letter to write before I took up my pen to put down what she wanted to dictate." The letter, she explained, which was difficult to write, was to her husband. She would feel easier when it was written. For her husband she expressed so much affection, that the doctor, knowing what had passed, felt much surprised, and wishing to try her, said that the affection was not reciprocated, as her husband had abandoned her the whole time of the trial. The marquise interrupted him:

"My father, we must not judge things too quickly or merely by appearances. M. de Brinvilliers has always concerned himself with me, and has only failed in doing what it was impossible to do. Our interchange of letters never ceased while I was out of the kingdom; do not doubt but that he would have come to Paris as soon as he knew I was in prison, had the state of his affairs allowed him to come safely. But you must know that he is deeply in debt, and could not appear in Paris without being arrested. Do not suppose that he is without feeling for me."

She then began to write, and when her letter was finished she handed it to the doctor, saying, "You, sir, are the lord and master of all my sentiments from now till I die; read this letter, and if you find anything that should be altered, tell me."

This was the letter—

"When I am on the point of yielding up my soul to God, I wish to assure you of my affection for you, which I shall feel until the last moment of my life. I ask your pardon for all that I have done contrary to my duty. I am dying a shameful death, the work of my enemies: I pardon them with all my heart, and I pray you to do the same. I also beg you to forgive me for any ignominy that may attach to you herefrom; but consider that we are only here for a time, and that you may soon be forced to render an account to God of all your actions, and even your idle words, just as I must do now. Be mindful of your worldly affairs, and of our children, and give them a good example; consult Madame Marillac and Madame Couste. Let as many prayers as possible be said for me, and believe that in my death I am still ever yours, D'AUBRAY."

The doctor read this letter carefully; then he told her that one of her phrases was not right—the one about her enemies. "For you have no other enemies," said he, "than your own crimes. Those whom you call your enemies are those who love the memory of your father and brothers, whom you ought to have loved more than they do."

"But those who have sought my death," she replied, "are my enemies, are they not, and is it not a Christian act to forgive them?"

"Madame," said the doctor, "they are not your enemies, but you are the enemy of the human race: nobody can think without, horror of your crimes."

"And so, my father," she replied, "I feel no resentment towards them, and I desire to meet in Paradise those who have been chiefly instrumental in taking me and bringing me here."

"Madame," said the doctor, "what mean you by this? Such words are used by some when they desire people's death. Explain, I beg, what you mean."

"Heaven forbid," cried the marquise, "that you should understand me thus! Nay, may God grant them long prosperity in this world and infinite glory in the next! Dictate a new letter, and I will write just what you please."

When a fresh letter had been written, the marquise would attend to nothing but her confession, and begged the doctor to take the pen for her. "I have done so many wrong thing's," she said, "that if I only gave you a verbal confession, I should never be sure I had given a complete account."

Then they both knelt down to implore the grace of the Holy Spirit. They said a 'Veni Creator' and a 'Salve Regina', and the doctor then rose and seated himself at a table, while the marquise, still on her knees, began a Confiteor and made her whole confession. At nine o'clock, Father Chavigny, who had brought Doctor Pirot in the morning, came in again. The marquise seemed annoyed, but still put a good face upon it. "My father," said she, "I did not expect to see you so late; pray leave me a few minutes longer with the doctor." He retired. " Why has he come?" asked the marquise.

"It is better for you not to be alone," said the doctor.

"Then do you mean to leave me?" cried the marquise, apparently terrified.

"Madame, I will do as you wish," he answered; "but you would be acting kindly if you could spare me for a few hours. I might go home, and Father Chavigny would stay with you."

"Ah!" she cried, wringing her hands, "you promised you would not leave me till I am dead, and now you go away. Remember, I never saw you before this morning, but since then you have become more to me than any of my oldest friends."

"Madame," said the good doctor, "I will do all I can to please you. If I ask for a little rest, it is in order that I may resume my place with more vigour to-morrow, and render you better service than I otherwise could. If I take no rest, all I say or do must suffer. You count on the execution for tomorrow; I do not know if you are right; but if so, to-morrow will be your great and decisive day, and we shall both need all the strength we have. We have already been working for thirteen or fourteen hours for the good of your salvation; I am not a strong man, and I think you should realise, madame, that if you do not let me rest a little, I may not be able to stay with you to the end."

"Sir," said the marquise, "you have closed my mouth. To-morrow is for me a far more important day than to-day, and I have been wrong: of course you must rest to-night. Let us just finish this one thing, and read over what we have written."

It was done, and the doctor would have retired; but the supper came in, and the marquise would not let him go without taking something. She told the concierge to get a carriage and charge it to her. She took a cup of soup and two eggs, and a minute later the concierge came back to say the carriage was at the door. Then the marquise bade the doctor good-night, making him promise to pray for her and to be at the Conciergerie by six o'clock the next morning. This he promised her.

The day following, as he went into the tower, he found Father Chavigny, who had taken his place with the marquise, kneeling and praying with her. The priest was weeping, but she was calm, and received the doctor in just the same way as she had let him go. When Father Chavigny saw him, he retired. The marquise begged Chavigny to pray for her, and wanted to make him promise to return, but that he would not do. She then turned to the doctor, saying, "Sir, you are punctual, and I cannot complain that you have broken your promise; but oh, how the time has dragged, and how long it has seemed before the clock struck six!"

"I am here, madame," said the doctor; "but first of all, how have you spent the night?"

"I have written three letters," said the marquise, "and, short as they were, they took a long time to write: one was to my sister, one to Madame de Marillac, and the third to M. Couste. I should have liked to show them to you, but Father Chavigny offered to take charge of them, and as he had approved of them, I could not venture to suggest any doubts. After the letters were written, we had some conversation and prayer; but when the father took up his breviary and I my rosary with the same intention, I felt so weary that I asked if I might lie on my bed; he said I might, and I had two good hours' sleep without dreams or any sort of uneasiness; when I woke we prayed together, and had just finished when you came back."

"Well, madame," said the doctor, "if you will, we can pray again; kneel down, and let us say the 'Veni Sancte Spiritus'."

She obeyed, and said the prayer with much unction and piety. The prayer finished, M. Pirot was about to take up the pen to go on with the confession, when she said, "Pray let me submit to you one question which is troubling me. Yesterday you gave me great hope of the mercy of God; but I cannot presume to hope I shall be saved without spending a long time in purgatory; my crime is far too atrocious to be pardoned on any other conditions; and when I have attained to a love of God far greater than I can feel here, I should not expect to be saved before my stains have been purified by fire, without suffering the penalty that my sins have deserved. But I have been told that the flames of purgatory where souls are burned for a time are just the same as the flames of hell where those who are damned burn through all eternity tell me, then, how can a soul awaking in purgatory at the moment of separation from this body be sure that she is not really in hell? how can she know that the flames that burn her and consume not will some day cease? For the torment she suffers is like that of the damned, and the flames wherewith she is burned are even as the flames of hell. This I would fain know, that at this awful moment I may feel no doubt, that I may know for certain whether I dare hope or must despair."

"Madame," replied the doctor, "you are right, and God is too just to add the horror of uncertainty to His rightful punishments. At that moment when the soul quits her earthly body the judgment of God is passed upon her: she hears the sentence of pardon or of doom; she knows whether she is in the state of grace or of mortal sin; she sees whether she is to be plunged forever into hell, or if God sends her for a time to purgatory. This sentence, madame, you will learn at the very instant when the executioner's axe strikes you; unless, indeed, the fire of charity has so purified you in this life that you may pass, without any purgatory at all, straight to the home of the blessed who surround the throne of the Lord, there to receive a recompense for earthly martyrdom."

"Sir," replied the marquise, "I have such faith in all you say that I feel I understand it all now, and I am satisfied."

The doctor and the marquise then resumed the confession that was interrupted the night before. The marquise had during the night recollected certain articles that she wanted to add. So they continued, the doctor making her pause now and then in the narration of the heavier offences to recite an act of contrition.

After an hour and a half they came to tell her to go down. The registrar was waiting to read her the sentence. She listened very calmly, kneeling, only moving her head; then, with no alteration in her voice, she said, "In a moment: we will have one word more, the doctor and I, and then I am at your disposal." She then continued to dictate the rest of her confession. When she reached the end, she begged him to offer a short prayer with her, that God might help her to appear with such becoming contrition before her judges as should atone for her scandalous effrontery. She then took up her cloak, a prayer-book which Father Chavigny had left with her, and followed the concierge, who led her to the torture chamber, where her sentence was to be read.

First, there was an examination which lasted five hours. The marquise told all she had promised to tell, denying that she had any accomplices, and affirming that she knew nothing of the composition of the poisons she had administered, and nothing of their antidotes. When this was done, and the judges saw that they could extract nothing further, they signed to the registrar to read the sentence. She stood to hear it: it was as follows:

"That by the finding of the court, d'Aubray de Brinvilliers is convicted of causing the death by poison of Maitre Dreux d'Aubray, her father, and of the two Maitres d'Aubray, her brothers, one a civil lieutenant, the other a councillor to the Parliament, also of attempting the life of Therese d'Aubray, her sister; in punishment whereof the court has condemned and does condemn the said d'Aubray de Brinvilliers to make the rightful atonement before the great gate of the church of Paris, whither she shall be conveyed in a tumbril, barefoot, a rope on her neck, holding in her hands a burning torch two pounds in weight; and there on her knees she shall say and declare that maliciously, with desire for revenge and seeking their goods, she did poison her father, cause to be poisoned her two brothers, and attempt the life of her sister, whereof she doth repent, asking pardon of God, of the king, and of the judges; and when this is done, she shall be conveyed and carried in the same tumbril to the Place de Greve of this town, there to have her head cut off on a scaffold to be set up for the purpose at that place; afterwards her body to be burnt and the ashes scattered; and first she is to be subjected to the question ordinary and extraordinary, that she may reveal the names of her accomplices. She is declared to be deprived of all successions from her said father, brothers, and sister, from the date of the several crimes; and all her goods are confiscated to the proper persons; and the sum of 4000 livres shall be paid out of her estate to the king, and 400 livres to the Church for prayers to be said on behalf of the poisoned persons; and all the costs shall be paid, including those of Amelin called Lachaussee. In Parliament, 16th July 1676."

The marquise heard her sentence without showing any sign of fear or weakness. When it was finished, she said to the registrar, " Will you, sir, be so kind as to read it again? I had not expected the tumbril, and I was so much struck by that that I lost the thread of what followed."

The registrar read the sentence again. From that moment she was the property of the executioner, who approached her. She knew him by the cord he held in his hands, and extended her own, looking him over coolly from head to foot without a word. The judges then filed out, disclosing as they did so the various apparatus of the question. The marquise firmly gazed upon the racks and ghastly rings, on which so many had been stretched crying and screaming. She noticed the three buckets of water

[Note: The torture with the water was thus administered. There were eight vessels, each containing 2 pints of water. Four of these were given for the ordinary, and eight for the extraordinary. The executioner inserted a horn into the patient's mouth, and if he shut his teeth, forced him to open them by pinching his nose with the finger and thumb.]

prepared for her, and turned to the registrar—for she would not address the executioner—saying, with a smile, "No doubt all this water is to drown me in? I hope you don't suppose that a person of my size could swallow it all." The executioner said not a word, but began taking off her cloak and all her other garments, until she was completely naked. He then led her up to the wall and made her sit on the rack of the ordinary question, two feet from the ground. There she was again asked to give the names of her accomplices, the composition of the poison and its antidote; but she made the same reply as to the doctor, only adding, "If you do not believe me, you have my body in your hands, and you can torture me."

The registrar signed to the executioner to do his duty. He first fastened the feet of the marquise to two rings close together fixed to a board; then making her lie down, he fastened her wrists to two other rings in the wall, distant about three feet from each other. The head was at the same height as the feet, and the body, held up on a trestle, described a half-curve, as though lying over a wheel. To increase the stretch of the limbs, the man gave two turns to a crank, which pushed the feet, at first about twelve inches from the rings, to a distance of six inches. And here we may leave our narrative to reproduce the official report.

"On the small trestle, while she was being stretched, she said several times, ' My God! you are killing me! And I only spoke the truth.'

"The water was given: she turned and twisted, saying, 'You are killing me!'

"The water was again given.

"Admonished to name her accomplices, she said there was only one man, who had asked her for poison to get rid of his wife, but he was dead.

"The water was given; she moved a little, but would not say anything.

"Admonished to say why, if she had no accomplice, she had written from the Conciergerie to Penautier, begging him to do all he could for her, and to remember that his interests in this matter were the same as her own, she said that she never knew Penautier had had any understanding with Sainte-Croix about the poisons, and it would be a lie to say otherwise; but when a paper was found in Sainte-Croix's box that concerned Penautier, she remembered how often she had seen him at the house, and thought it possible that the friendship might have included some business about the poisons;

that, being in doubt on the point, she risked writing a letter as though she were sure, for by doing so she was not prejudicing her own case; for either Penautier was an accomplice of Sainte-Croix or he was not. If he was, he would suppose the marquise knew enough to accuse him, and would accordingly do his best to save her; if he was not, the letter was a letter wasted, and that was all.

"The water was again given; she turned and twisted much, but said that on this subject she had said all she possibly could; if she said anything else, it would be untrue."

The ordinary question was at an end. The marquise had now taken half the quantity of water she had thought enough to drown her. The executioner paused before he proceeded to the extraordinary question. Instead of the trestle two feet and a half high on which she lay, they passed under her body a trestle of three and a half feet, which gave the body a greater arch, and as this was done without lengthening the ropes, her limbs were still further stretched, and the bonds, tightly straining at wrists and ankles, penetrated the flesh and made the blood run. The question began once more, interrupted by the demands of the registrar and the answers of the sufferer. Her cries seemed not even to be heard.

"On the large trestle, during the stretching, she said several times, 'O God, you tear me to, pieces! Lord, pardon me! Lord, have mercy upon me!'

"Asked if she had nothing more to tell regarding her accomplices, she said they might kill her, but she would not tell a lie that would destroy her soul.

"The water was given, she moved about a little, but would not speak.

"Admonished that she should tell the composition of the poisons and their antidotes, she said that she did not know what was in them; the only thing she could recall was toads; that Sainte-Croix never revealed his secret to her; that she did not believe he made them himself, but had them prepared by Glazer; she seemed to remember that some of them contained nothing but rarefied arsenic; that as to an antidote, she knew of no other than milk; and Sainte-Croix had told her that if one had taken milk in the morning, and on the first onset of the poison took another glassful, one would have nothing to fear.

"Admonished to say if she could add anything further, she said she had now told everything; and if they killed her, they could not extract anything more.

"More water was given; she writhed a little, and said she was dead, but nothing more.

"More water was given; she writhed more violently, but would say no more.

"Yet again water was given; writhing and twisting, she said, with a deep groan, 'O my God, I am killed!' but would speak no more."

Then they tortured her no further: she was let down, untied, and placed before the fire in the usual manner. While there, close to the fire, lying on the mattress, she was visited by the good doctor, who, feeling he could not bear to witness the spectacle just described, had asked her leave to retire, that he might say a mass for her, that God might grant her patience and courage. It is plain that the good priest had not prayed in vain.

"Ah," said the marquise, when she perceived him, "I have long been desiring to see you again, that you might comfort me. My torture has been very long and very painful, but this is the last time I shall have to treat with men; now all is with God for the future. See my hands, sir, and my feet, are they not torn and wounded? Have not my executioners smitten me in the same places where Christ was smitten?"

"And therefore, madame," replied the priest, "these sufferings now are your happiness; each torture is one step nearer to heaven. As you say, you are now for God alone; all your thoughts and hopes must be fastened upon Him; we must pray to Him, like the penitent king, to give you a place among His elect; and since nought that is impure can pass thither, we must strive, madame, to purify you from all that might bar the way to heaven."

The marquise rose with the doctor's aid, for she could scarcely stand; tottering, she stepped forward between him and the executioner, who took charge of her immediately after the sentence was read, and was not allowed to leave her before it was completely carried out. They all three entered the chapel and went into the choir, where the doctor and the marquise knelt in adoration of the Blessed Sacrament. At that moment several persons appeared in the nave, drawn by curiosity. They could not be turned out, so the executioner, to save the marquise from being annoyed, shut the gate of the choir, and let the patient pass behind the altar. There she sat down in a chair, and the doctor on a seat opposite; then he first saw, by the light of the chapel window, how greatly changed she was. Her face, generally so pale, was inflamed, her eyes glowing and feverish, all her body involuntarily trembling. The doctor would have spoken a few words of consolation, but she did not attend. "Sir," she said, "do you know that my sentence is an ignominious one? Do you know there is fire in the sentence?"

The doctor gave no answer; but, thinking she needed something, bade the gaoler to bring her wine. A minute later he brought it in a cup, and the doctor handed it to the marquise, who moistened her lips and then gave it back. She then noticed that her neck was uncovered, and took out her handkerchief to cover it, asking the gaoler for a pin to fasten it with. When he was slow in finding a pin, looking on his person for it, she fancied that he feared she would choke herself, and shaking her head, said, with a smile, "You have nothing to fear now; and here is the doctor, who will pledge his word that I will do myself no mischief."

"Madame," said the gaoler, handing her the pin she wanted, "I beg your pardon for keeping you waiting. I swear I did not distrust you; if anyone distrusts you, it is not I."

Then kneeling before her, he begged to kiss her hand. She gave it, and asked him to pray to God for her. "Ah yes," he cried, sobbing, "with all my heart." She then fastened her dress as best she could with her hands tied, and when the gaoler had gone and she was alone with the doctor, said:—

"Did you not hear what I said, sir? I told you there was fire in my sentence. And though it is only after death that my body is to be burnt, it will always be a terrible disgrace on my memory. I am saved the pain of being burnt alive, and thus, perhaps, saved from a death of despair, but the shamefulness is the same, and it is that I think of."

"Madame," said the doctor, "it in no way affects your soul's salvation whether your body is cast into the fire and reduced to ashes or whether it is buried in the ground and eaten by worms, whether it is drawn on a hurdle and thrown upon a dung-heap, or embalmed with Oriental perfumes and laid in a rich man's tomb. Whatever may be your end, your body will arise on the appointed day, and if Heaven so will, it will come forth from its ashes more glorious than a royal corpse lying at this moment in a gilded casket. Obsequies, madame, are for those who survive, not for the dead."

A sound was heard at the door of the choir. The doctor went to see what it was, and found a man who insisted on entering, all but fighting with the executioner. The doctor approached and asked what was the matter. The man was a saddler, from whom the marquise had bought a carriage before she left France; this she had partly paid for, but still owed him two hundred livres. He produced the note he had had from her, on which was a faithful record of the sums she had paid on account. The marquise at this point called out, not knowing what was going on, and the doctor and executioner went to her. "Have they come to fetch me already?" said she. "I am not well prepared just at this moment; but never mind, I am ready."

The doctor reassured her, and told her what was going on. "The man is quite right," she said to the executioner; " tell him I will give orders as far as I can about the money." Then, seeing the executioner retiring, she said to the doctor, " Must I go now, sir? I wish they would give me a little more time; for though I am ready, as I told you, I am not really prepared. Forgive me, father; it is the question and the sentence that have upset me it is this fire burning in my eyes like hell-flames.

Had they left me with you all this time, there would now be better hope of my salvation."

"Madame," said the doctor, "you will probably have all the time before nightfall to compose yourself and think what remains for you to do."

"Ah, sir," she replied, with a smile, "do not think they will show so much consideration for a poor wretch condemned to be burnt. That does not depend on ourselves; but as soon as everything is ready, they will let us know, and we must start."

"Madame," said the doctor, "I am certain that they will give you the time you need."

"No, no," she replied abruptly and feverishly, "no, I will not keep them waiting. As soon as the tumbril is at this door, they have only to tell me, and I go down."

"Madame," said he, "I would not hold you back if I found you prepared to stand before the face of God, for in your situation it is right to ask for no time, and to go when the moment is come; but not everyone is so ready as Christ was, who rose from prayer and awaked His disciples that He might leave the garden and go out to meet His enemies. You at this moment are weak, and if they come for you just now I should resist your departure."

"Be calm; the time is not yet come," said the executioner, who had heard this talk. He knew his statement must be believed, and wished as far as possible to reassure the marquise. "There is no hurry, and we cannot start for another two of three hours."

This assurance calmed the marquise somewhat, and she thanked the man. Then turning to the doctor, she said, "Here is a rosary that I would rather should not fall into this person's hands. Not that he could not make good use of it; for, in spite of their trade, I fancy that these people are Christians like ourselves. But I should prefer to leave this to somebody else."

"Madame," said the doctor, "if you will tell me your wishes in this matter, I will see that they are carried out."

"Alas!" she said, "there is no one but my sister; and I fear lest she, remembering my crime towards her, may be too horrified to touch anything that belonged to me. If she did not mind, it would be a great comfort to me to think she would wear it after my death, and that the sight of it would remind her to pray for me; but after what has passed, the rosary could hardly fail to revive an odious recollection. My God, my God! I am desperately wicked; can it be that you will pardon me?"

"Madame," replied the doctor, "I think you are mistaken about Mlle, d'Aubray. You may see by her letter what are her feelings towards you, and you must pray with this rosary up to the very end. Let not your prayers be interrupted or distracted, for no guilty penitent must cease from prayer; and I, madame, will engage to deliver the rosary where it will be gladly received."

And the marquise, who had been constantly distracted since the morning, was now, thanks to the patient goodness of the doctor, able to return with her former fervour to her prayers. She prayed till seven o'clock. As the clock struck, the executioner without a word came and stood before her; she saw that her moment had come, and said to the doctor, grasping his arm, "A little longer; just a few moments, I entreat."

"Madame," said the doctor, rising, "we will now adore the divine blood of the Sacrament, praying that you may be thus cleansed from all soil and sin that may be still in your heart. Thus shall you gain the respite you desire."

The executioner then tied tight the cords round her hands that he had let loose before, and she advanced pretty firmly and knelt before the altar, between the doctor and the chaplain. The latter was in his surplice, and chanted a 'Veni Creator, Salve Regina, and Tantum ergo'. These prayers over, he pronounced the blessing of the Holy Sacrament, while the marquise knelt with her face upon the ground. The executioner then went forward to get ready a shirt, and she made her exit from the chapel, supported on the left by the doctor's arm, on the right by the executioner's assistant. Thus proceeding, she first felt embarrassment and confusion. Ten or twelve people were waiting outside, and as she suddenly confronted them, she made a step backward, and with her hands, bound though they were, pulled the headdress down to cover half her face. She passed through a small door, which was closed behind her, and then found herself between the two doors alone, with the doctor and the executioner's man. Here the rosary, in consequence of her violent movement to cover her face, came undone, and several beads fell on the floor. She went on, however, without observing this; but the doctor stopped her, and he and the man stooped down and picked up all the beads, which they put into her hand. Thanking them humbly for this attention, she said to the man, "Sir, I know I have now no worldly possessions, that all I have upon me belongs to you, and I may not give anything away without your consent; but I ask you kindly to allow me to give this chaplet to the doctor before I die: you will not be much the loser, for it is of no value, and I am giving it to him for my sister. Kindly let me do this."

"Madame," said the man, "it is the custom for us to get all the property of the condemned; but you are mistress of all you have, and if the thing were of the very greatest value you might dispose of it as you pleased."

The doctor, whose arm she held, felt her shiver at this gallantry, which for her, with her natural haughty disposition, must have been the worst humiliation imaginable; but the movement was restrained, and her face gave no sign. She now came to the porch of the Conciergerie, between the court and the first door, and there she was made to sit down, so as to be put into the right condition for making the 'amende honorable'. Each step brought her nearer to the scaffold, and so did each incident cause her more uneasiness. Now she turned round desperately, and perceived the executioner holding a shirt in his hand. The door of the vestibule opened, and about fifty people came in, among them the Countess of Soissons, Madame du Refuge, Mlle. de Scudery, M, de Roquelaure, and the Abbe de Chimay. At the sight the marquise reddened with shame, and turning to the doctor, said, "Is this man to strip me again, as he did in the question chamber? All these preparations are very cruel; and, in spite of myself, they divert my thoughts, from God."

Low as her voice was, the executioner heard, and reassured her, saying that they would take nothing off, only putting the shirt over her other clothes.

He then approached, and the marquise, unable to speak to the doctor with a man on each side of her, showed him by her looks how deeply she felt the ignominy of her situation. Then, when the shirt had been put on, for which operation her hands had to be untied, the man raised the headdress which she had pulled down, and tied it round her neck, then fastened her hands together with one rope and put another round her waist, and yet another round her neck; then, kneeling before her, he took off her shoes and stockings. Then she stretched out her hands to the doctor.

"Oh, sir," she cried, "in God's name, you see what they have done to me! Come and comfort me."

The doctor came at once, supporting her head upon his breast, trying to comfort her; but she, in a tone of bitter lamentation, gazing at the crowd, who devoured her with all their eyes, cried, "Oh, sir, is not this a strange, barbarous curiosity?"

"Madame," said he, the tears in his eyes, "do not look at these eager people from the point of view of their curiosity and barbarity, though that is real enough, but consider it part of the humiliation sent by God for the expiation of your crimes. God, who was innocent, was subject to very different opprobrium, and yet suffered all with joy; for, as Tertullian observes, He was a victim fattened on the joys of suffering alone."

As the doctor spoke these words, the executioner placed in the marquise's hands the lighted torch which she was to carry to Notre-Dame, there to make the 'amende honorable', and as it was too heavy, weighing two pounds, the doctor supported it with his right hand, while the registrar read her sentence aloud a second time. The doctor did all in his power to prevent her from hearing this by speaking unceasingly of God. Still she grew frightfully pale at the words, "When this is done, she shall be conveyed on a tumbril, barefoot, a cord round her neck, holding in her hands a burning torch two pounds in weight," and the doctor could feel no doubt that in spite of his efforts she had heard. It became still worse when she reached the threshold of the vestibule and saw the great crowd waiting in the court. Then her face worked convulsively, and crouching down, as though she would bury her feet in the earth, she addressed the doctor in words both plaintive and wild: "Is it possible that, after what is now happening, M. de Brinvilliers can endure to go on living?"

"Madame," said the doctor, "when our Lord was about to leave His disciples, He did not ask God to remove them from this earth, but to preserve them from all sin. 'My Father,' He said, 'I ask not that You take them from the world, but keep them safe from evil.' If, madame, you pray for M. de Brinvilliers, let it be only that he may be kept in grace, if he has it, and may attain to it if he has it not."

But the words were useless: at that moment the humiliation was too great and too public; her face contracted, her eyebrows knit, flames darted from her eyes, her mouth was all twisted. Her whole appearance was horrible; the devil was once more in possession. During this paroxysm, which lasted nearly a quarter of an hour, Lebrun, who stood near, got such a vivid impression of her face that the following night he could not sleep, and with the sight of it ever before his eyes made the fine drawing which—is now in the Louvre, giving to the figure the head of a tiger, in order to show that the principal features were the same, and the whole resemblance very striking.

The delay in progress was caused by the immense crowd blocking the court, only pushed aside by archers on horseback, who separated the people. The marquise now went out, and the doctor, lest the sight of the people should completely distract her, put a crucifix in her hand, bidding her fix her gaze upon it. This advice she followed till they gained the gate into the street where the tumbril was waiting; then she lifted her eyes to see the shameful object. It was one of the smallest of carts, still splashed with mud and marked by the stones it had carried, with no seat, only a little straw at the bottom. It was drawn by a wretched horse, well matching the disgraceful conveyance.

The executioner bade her get in first, which she did very rapidly, as if to escape observation. There she crouched like a wild beast, in the left corner, on the straw, riding backwards. The doctor sat beside her on the right. Then the executioner got in, shutting the door behind him, and sat opposite her, stretching his legs between the doctor's. His man, whose business it was to guide the horse, sat on the front, back to back with the doctor and the marquise, his feet stuck out on the shafts. Thus it is easy to understand how Madame de Sevigne, who was on the Pont Notre-Dame, could see nothing but the headdress of the marquise as she was driven to Notre-Dame.

The cortege had only gone a few steps, when the face of the marquise, for a time a little calmer, was again convulsed. From her eyes, fixed constantly on the crucifix, there darted a flaming glance, then came a troubled and frenzied look which terrified the doctor. He knew she must have been struck by something she saw, and, wishing to calm her, asked what it was.

"Nothing, nothing," she replied quickly, looking towards him; "it was nothing."

"But, madame," said he, "you cannot give the lie to your own eyes; and a minute ago I saw a fire very different from the fire of love, which only some displeasing sight can have provoked. What may this be? Tell me, pray; for you promised to tell me of any sort of temptation that might assail you."

"Sir," she said, "I will do so, but it is nothing." Then, looking towards the executioner, who, as we know, sat facing the doctor, she said, "Put me in front of you, please; hide that man from me." And she stretched out her hands towards a man who was following the tumbril on horseback, and so dropped the torch, which the doctor took, and the crucifix, which fell on the floor. The executioner looked back, and then turned sideways as she wished, nodding and saying, "Oh yes, I understand." The doctor pressed to know what it meant, and she said, "It is nothing worth telling you, and it is a weakness in me not to be able to bear the sight of a man who has ill- used me. The man who touched the back of the tumbril is Desgrais, who arrested me at Liege, and treated me so badly all along the road. When I saw him, I could not control myself, as you noticed."

"Madame," said the doctor, "I have heard of him, and you yourself spoke of him in confession; but the man was sent to arrest you, and was in a responsible position, so that he had to guard you closely and rigorously; even if he had been more severe, he would only have been carrying out his orders. Jesus Christ, madame, could but have regarded His executioners as ministers of iniquity, servants of injustice, who added of their own accord every indignity they could think of; yet all along the way He looked on them with patience and more than patience, and in His death He prayed for them."

In the heart of the marquise a hard struggle was passing, and this was reflected on her face; but it was only for a moment, and after a last convulsive shudder she was again calm and serene; then she said: —

"Sir, you are right, and I am very wrong to feel such a fancy as this: may God forgive me; and pray remember this fault on the scaffold, when you give me the absolution you promise, that this too may be pardoned me." Then she turned to the executioner and said, "Please sit where you were before, that I may see M. Desgrais." The man hesitated, but on a sign from the doctor obeyed. The marquise looked fully at Desgrais for some time, praying for him; then, fixing her eyes on the crucifix, began to pray for herself: this incident occurred in front of the church of Sainte-Genevieve des Ardents.

But, slowly as it moved, the tumbril steadily advanced, and at last reached the place of Notre-Dame. The archers drove back the crowding people, and the tumbril went up to the steps, and there stopped. The executioner got down, removed the board at the back, held out his arms to the marquise, and set her down on the pavement. The doctor then got down, his legs quite numb from the cramped position he had been in since they left the Conciergerie. He mounted the church steps and stood behind the marquise, who herself stood on the square, with the registrar on her right, the executioner on her left, and a great crowd of people behind her, inside the church, all the doors being thrown open. She was made to kneel, and in her hands was placed the lighted torch, which up to that time the doctor had helped to carry. Then the registrar read the 'amende honorable' from a written paper, and she began to say it after him, but in so low a voice that the executioner said loudly, "Speak out as he does; repeat every word. Louder, louder!" Then she raised her voice, and loudly and firmly recited the following apology.

"I confess that, wickedly and for revenge, I poisoned my father and my brothers, and attempted to poison my sister, to obtain possession of their goods, and I ask pardon of God, of the king, and of my country's laws."

The 'amende honorable' over, the executioner again carried her to the tumbril, not giving her the torch any more: the doctor sat beside her: all was just as before, and the tumbril went on towards La Greve. From that moment, until she arrived at the scaffold, she never took her eyes off the crucifix, which the doctor held before her the whole time, exhorting her with religious words, trying to divert her attention from the terrible noise which the people made around the car, a murmur mingled with curses.

When they reached the Place de Greve, the tumbril stopped at a little distance from the scaffold. Then the registrar M. Drouet, came up on horseback, and, addressing the marquise, said, "Madame, have you nothing more to say? If you wish to make any declaration, the twelve commissaries are here at hand, ready to receive it."

"You see, madame," said the doctor, "we are now at the end of our journey, and, thank God, you have not lost your power of endurance on the road; do not destroy the effect of all you have suffered and all you have yet to suffer by concealing what you know, if perchance you do know more than you have hitherto said."

"I have told all I know," said the marquise, "and there is no more I can say."

"Repeat these words in a loud voice," said the doctor, "so that everybody may hear."

Then in her loudest voice the marquise repeated —

"I have told all I know, and there is no more I can say."

After this declaration, they were going to drive the tumbril nearer to the scaffold, but the crowd was so dense that the assistant could not force a way through, though he struck out on every side with his whip. So they had to stop a few paces short. The executioner had already got down, and was adjusting the ladder. In this terrible moment of waiting, the marquise looked calmly and gratefully at the doctor, and when she felt that the tumbril had stopped, said, "Sir, it is not here we part: you promised not to leave me till my head is cut off. I trust you will keep your word."

"To be sure I will," the doctor replied; "we shall not be separated before the moment of your death: be not troubled about that, for I will never forsake you."

"I looked for this kindness," she said, "and your promise was too solemn for you to think for one moment of failing me. Please be on the scaffold and be near me. And now, sir, I would anticipate the final farewell,—for all the things I shall have to do on the scaffold may distract me,—so let me thank you here. If I am prepared to suffer the sentence of my earthly judge, and to hear that of my heavenly judge, I owe it to your care for me, and I am deeply grateful. I can only ask your forgiveness for the trouble I have given you." Tears choked the doctor's speech, and he could not reply. "Do you not forgive me?" she repeated. At her words, the doctor tried to reassure her; but feeling that if he opened his mouth he must needs break into sobs, he still kept silent. The marquise appealed to him a third time. "I entreat you, sir, forgive me; and do not regret the time you have passed with me. You will say a De Profundus at the moment of my death, and a mass far me to-morrow: will you not promise?"

"Yes, madame," said the doctor in a choking voice; "yes, yes, be calm, and I will do all you bid me."

The executioner hereupon removed the board, and helped the marquise out of the tumbril; and as they advanced the few steps towards the scaffold, and all eyes were upon them, the doctor could hide his tears for a moment without being observed. As he was drying his eyes, the assistant gave him his hand to help him down. Meanwhile the marquise was mounting the ladder with the executioner, and when they reached the platform he told her to kneel down in front of a block which lay across it. Then the doctor, who had mounted with a step less firm than hers, came and knelt beside her, but turned in the other direction, so that he might whisper in her ear—that is, the marquise faced the river, and the doctor faced the Hotel de Ville. Scarcely had they taken their place thus when the man took down her hair and began cutting it at the back and at the sides, making her turn her head this way and that, at times rather roughly; but though this ghastly toilet lasted almost half an hour, she made no complaint, nor gave any sign of pain but her silent tears. When her hair was cut, he tore open the top of the shirt, so as to uncover the shoulders, and finally bandaged her eyes, and lifting her face by the chin, ordered her to hold her head erect. She obeyed, unresisting, all the time listening to the doctor's words and repeating them from time to time, when they seemed suitable to her own condition. Meanwhile, at the back of the scaffold, on which the stake was placed, stood the executioner, glancing now and again at the folds of his cloak, where there showed the hilt of a long, straight sabre, which he had carefully concealed for fear Madame de Brinvilliers might see it when she mounted the scaffold. When the doctor, having pronounced absolution, turned his head and saw that the man was not yet armed, he uttered these prayers, which she repeated after him: "Jesus, Son of David and Mary, have mercy upon me; Mary, daughter of David and Mother of Jesus, pray for me; my God, I abandon my body, which is but dust, that men may burn it and do with it what they please, in the firm faith that it shall one day arise and be reunited with my soul. I trouble not concerning my body; grant, O God, that I yield up to Thee my soul, that it may enter into Thy rest; receive it into Thy bosom; that it may dwell once more there, whence it first descended; from Thee it came, to Thee returns; Thou art the source and the beginning; be thou, O God, the centre and the end!"

The marquise had said these words when suddenly the doctor heard a dull stroke like the sound of a chopper chopping meat upon a block: at that moment she ceased to speak. The blade had sped so quickly that the doctor had not even seen a flash. He stopped, his hair bristling, his brow bathed in sweat; for, not seeing the head fall, he supposed that the executioner had missed the mark and must needs start afresh. But his fear was short-lived, for almost at the same moment the head inclined to the left, slid on to the shoulder, and thence backward, while the body fell forward on the crossway block, supported so that the spectators could see the neck cut open and bleeding. Immediately, in fulfilment of his promise, the doctor said a De Profundis.

When the prayer was done and the doctor raised his head, he saw before him the executioner wiping his face. "Well, sir," said he, "was not that a good stroke? I always put up a prayer on these occasions, and God has always assisted me; but I have been anxious for several days about this lady. I had six masses said, and I felt strengthened in hand and heart." He then pulled out a bottle from under his cloak, and drank a dram; and taking the body under one arm, all dressed as it was, and the head in his other hand, the eyes still bandaged, he threw both upon the faggots, which his assistant lighted.

"The next day," says Madame de Sevigne, "people were looking for the charred bones of Madame de Brinvilliers, because they said she was a saint."

In 1814, M. d'Offemont, father of the present occupier of the castle where the Marquise de Brinvilliers poisoned her father, frightened at the approach of all the allied troops, contrived in one of the towers several hiding-places, where he shut up his silver and such other valuables as were to be found in this lonely country in the midst of the forest of Laigue. The foreign troops were passing backwards and forwards at Offemont, and after a three months' occupation retired to the farther side of the frontier.

Then the owners ventured to take out the various things that had been hidden; and tapping the walls, to make sure nothing had been overlooked, they detected a hollow sound that indicated the presence of some unsuspected cavity. With picks and bars they broke the wall open, and when several stones had come out they found a large closet like a laboratory, containing furnaces, chemical instruments, phials hermetically sealed full of an unknown liquid, and four packets of powders of different colours. Unluckily, the people who made these discoveries thought them of too much or too little importance; and instead of submitting the ingredients to the tests of modern science, they made away with them all, frightened at their probably deadly nature.

Thus was lost this great opportunity—probably the last—for finding and analysing the substances which composed the poisons of Sainte-Croix and Madame de Brinvilliers.

End

CPSIA information can be obtained at www.ICGtesting.com
Printed in the USA
BVOW080040151112

305525BV00003B/339/P